BLACK
WRITERS
UNMASKED

AFRICAN-AMERICAN WRITERS' ALLIANCE
SEATTLE, WASHINGTON

Creative Commons licensing: Attribution, Non-Commercial, Share Alike

Anthology, Fiction, Nonfiction, Poetry

Printed in the United States of America
Compiled by Dr. Georgia S. McDade and Minnie Collins
Layout design by Lola E Peters
Cover art #264624393 from Adobe Stock Photos
The African-American Writers' Alliance is a 501(c)3 non-profit organization under the fiscal sponsorship of Shunpike. Shunpike empowers artists through equitable access to vital expertise, opportunities, and business services.

ISBN# 979-8-9857008-0-0

African-American Writers' Alliance
c/o Shunpike
815 Seattle Blvd S Ste 215
Seattle, WA 98134 US

TABLE OF CONTENTS

FOREWORD VI
INTRODUCTION VII
ACKNOWLEDGEMENTS VIII
BLACK WRITERS UNMASKED 2
   KATHYA ALEXANDER 3
      Naa Naa 4
   MARGARET S. BARRIE 9
      A Glimpse of the Universe 10
      Anywhere Cityscape 11
      Autumn Birch 12
      Winter Birch 12
      Essence 12
      A Life Ending 13
      True Love 14
      The Fall 15
   HELEN J. COLLIER 17
      Willie the Blacksmith 18
      A Letter from the Past: Klan Race Riots 24
      Too Late 25
      Daybreak 26
      Go Back to Africa 26
      Excerpt from Ms. Anna The Promise Keeper 27
   MINNIE A. COLLINS 29
      Layered Lies 30
      Revolutionary Dialogue 30
      Troubled Waters 31
   NONI ERVIN 35
      Celebrating You 36
      Gratitude Freestyle 37
      Lifelong Friends 38
      Cannonballs 39
      Rest in Peace 41
   MIZ PORTIONTÉ FLOES 43
      Red White & Black! 44
      Blackness Interrupted 47
      IT'S TIME TO GROW 50
   TRACI HARRELL 53
      Transformational Inclusive Leadership, with Mind, Heart & Soul 54

GAIL HAYNES 61
   Coming to Jesus Out of the Ditch 62
LEOMA JAMES 65
   Pacific Place 66
   Understood 67
GEORGIA STEWART MCDADE 69
   The Greens 70
   Two for One 70
   The Cranes 71
   What Raffles Wrought 72
NANA KIBIBI MONIÉ 75
   Twinkle, Twinkle Little Rat 76
   The Inventors Rap 77
   I Am African 79
   I'M SUPPOSED TO BE FREE! 81
ROLYAT MOSI 83
   Ali Passed by My Window 84
   Thanksgiving with No Turkey 87
   Concrete Roses 92
   Creator Queen 93
MERRI ANN OSBORNE 95
   Unrecognizable 96
   Zahara Goes to Summer Camp 99
   Humidity 107
LOLA E. PETERS 109
   Never Ending 110
   Grace 110
   My Space 111
   A Lost Diamond of the Patriarchal Society 112
   Spring Blossoms 113
   Prequel 114
   Breathe, Children, Breathe 115
   Inside the Cave 117
   Branded 118
   Dark Matter 119
   ReEvolution 121
DELBERT RICHARDSON 123
   We Gonna Be Free 124
   When All Lives Matter 125
GAYLLOYD SISSÓN 127
   Spiders in My Yard 128
   A Roach 129

- *My Son and Me* *131*
- *War* *132*
- *Enjoy Nature* *132*
- *Yoga* *133*
- *Nature Chatters* *134*
- *Ocean Beaches* *135*
- *The Weeds Are Winning* *137*
- *Life* *137*
- *What to Do?* *138*
- *Extinction* *139*
- *Your Name Is Love* *140*
- *Arise from the Dead* *141*

Yvonne Smith 145
- *Motion-less of Life* *146*
- *When We Were Free* *147*
- *What If Tomorrow Never Comes?* *148*

Jacqueline (Jaye) Ware 149
- *About that Love* *150*
- *Black Identity* *152*
- *"WE HAVE BROUGHT PEACE TO THE WORLD"* *154*
- *Matted Queen* *156*

Reginald "Doc" Williams 159
- *This Used to Be a Nice Street* *160*
- *Let Them Be* *160*
- *Christmas* *160*
- *Just Another Dead Nigger* *161*
- *9/11* *162*

FOREWORD

This anthology from the African-American Writers' Alliance is a gift for readers and for the writers themselves. The creation and consumption of written words are both enriching endeavors. Reading and writing both help us learn about ourselves and the world around us.

The Alliance has been nurturing Black writers since its founding in 1991 and encouraging them to share what they create with the broader community. The writers come from many walks of life, and most don't write for a living, but rather out of a passion for exploration and communication.

Every reader will find someone to connect with within this collection. I found several.

The first piece in the book, "Naa Naa," by the storyteller Kathya Alexander evoked memories of my mother rising early and picking cotton under a broiling sun. Minnie A. Collins held my attention with a poem on the transformative power of revolution, then in a short story that captures the feel of domestic frustration.

Georgia S. McDade, who joined the alliance in 1991 and is its animating force, is represented here as well. I especially appreciated her nonfiction piece on a decades-long friendship that began with her trusting a stranger and holding onto friendship despite their differences.

I enjoyed the thought-provoking poems of Lola E. Peters, including one in which the speaker is seeking a space in which she can just be.

These writers have found one such space in this special collection.

Jerry Large
Retired columnist, *The Seattle Times*
December 2021

INTRODUCTION

The African-American Writers' Alliance (AAWA) was founded in 1991 by Californian Randee Eddins. She encouraged an exchange of ideas, works in progress, and sharing our poems, stories, essays, plays, and novels. In this mutually supportive setting, writers listened and shared their work without censure.

AAWA is a diverse and dynamic collective of Seattle-area writers of African descent that provides an informal and supportive forum for new and published writers. We help one another polish our skills, provide peer review, and create opportunities for public readings and other media venues. Ultimately the group encourages members to publish individually and collectively. Our stories—triumphs, tragedies, and whatever is within and between the two—are the history of African Americans.

The poems, short stories, essays, and reflections contained in this volume reflect the diversity of seldom heard voices, perspectives, experiences, and skills existing throughout our Pacific Northwest communities of African descent. Some are veteran writers; some are just developing their craft. All are passionate about their work and eager to share with readers.

AAWA is proud to present them and proud to create space to amplify their self-expression. We must tell our stories in our words and encourage others to do the same.

AAWA has published five previous anthologies: *Sometimes I Wander* in 1998, *Gifted Voices* in 2000, *Words? Words! Words* in 2004, *Threads* in 2009, and *Voices That Matter* in 2018.

ACKNOWLEDGEMENTS

AAWA extends special, heartfelt, thanks to the many partners who have given us voice over the years:

- Ms. Randee Eddins, who founded AAWA in 1991 and created a space for Black writers to be seen and heard where there was none.
- Dr. Georgia Stewart McDade, who has kept AAWA alive and thriving Outside the Cave (the title of her four books of poetry).
- Elliott Bay Book Co. for giving us their stage on the last week of February each year for 31 years. Special thanks to Rick Simonson for his unwavering belief in our mission.
- Onyx Fine Arts Collective for inviting AAWA to write ekphrastic poems in response to their annual juried exhibits every year since 2009.
- The Seattle Art Museum for inviting AAWA to write ekphrastic poems in response to featured exhibits in 1992, 2004, and 2021.
- Seattle Public Library and Seattle Library Foundation for incorporating AAWA in its Seattle Reads and Summer of Learning projects, supporting our books and readings, and providing us a consistent home at the Columbia City Library.
- Ballard Branch of the Seattle Public Library for inviting AAWA writers to read at featured events.
- Poets West, especially Art Gomez, for supporting AAWA's readings and becoming an extended part of the AAWA family.
- Open Books: A Poetry Emporium in Wallingford for featuring AAWA poets and books.
- Third Place Books in Seward Park for hosting AAWA's monthly readings.
- Gallery 110 (Seattle), Humble Vine (Burien), Bin 41 (West Seattle), Highline Heritage Museum (Burien), and many others who have incorporated AAWA into their arts programs.
- Shunpike, which provides many arts organizations with fiscal and institutional support, enabling us to focus on our mission.
- Seattle's Office of Arts & Culture and King County's 4Culture for programs like ACES and their arts funding programs.

We also profoundly thank you, our donors, readers, and supporters who have participated in our monthly Writers' Read program at the Columbia City Library, come to many of our events, encouraged the new writers among us and appreciated the variety of voices, styles, subjects, and points of view within our community. Most of all, we thank our members, who trust each other with our fragile work and show us the pathways available to developing our writing art and craft.

We invite readers to visit AAWA's website (www.aawa-seattle.org) to learn more about AAWA's history, each of our members, upcoming readings and events, how to become a member, and how to continue to support our work.

To read more from AAWA's writers, check out our previous anthologies: *Sometimes I Wander* (1998), *Gifted Voices* (2000), *Words? Words! Words* (2004), *Threads* (2009), and *Voices That Matter* (2018).

Thank you all for your support,

AAWA's 2022 Leadership Council
Dr. Georgia S. McDade, Charter Member
Helen Collier & Gaylloyd Sissón, Co-chairs
Margaret Barrie, Treasurer
Noni Ervin, Secretary

Annual reading at Elliott Bay Book Co. 2018

Front Row: Gail Haynes, Jaye Ware, Margaret Barrie, Helen Collier, Minnie Collins
Back Row: Kilam Tel Aviv, Gaylloyd Sissón, Santiago Vega, Imhotep Ptah, Lola Peters

Annual reading at Elliott Bay Book Co. 2022

BLACK WRITERS UNMASKED

KATHYA ALEXANDER is a writer, actor, storyteller, and teaching artist. Her writing has appeared in the *South Seattle Emerald*, *ColorsNW Magazine*, *Arkana Magazine*, *Native Skin*, *Raising Lilly Ledbetter*, and *The Pitkin Review*. She has won the Artist Trust GAP Award, Jack Straw Artist Support Program Award, 4Culture's Artists Projects Award, the WRAP Award, Youth Arts Award, and the CityArtist Award from Seattle's Office of Arts and Culture. Her play "HomeGoing" was chosen for residency at Hedgebrook Women's Writer's Retreat; her play "Black To My Roots: African-American Tales from the Head and the Heart" won the Edinburgh Festival Fringe First Award in Edinburgh, Scotland for Outstanding New Production. Her collection of short stories, *Angel in the Outhouse*, is available on Amazon.

Naa Naa

She wake up in the blackness. The darkest hour of the day.
Just before the Lord come and roll the nighttime away.
She the color of night. Her skin stretched tight
across her face. And the veins on her hands tell the whole story of
    her life.
She sit on the slop jar by the bed. She careful not to wake
the sleeping body beside her, Miz Irma, her housemate.
She ain't never been married. Never had chick nor child.
Miz Irma is the only kinda family she got.
Beside us, that is. We not blood or nothing neither.
But Mama say she help them when they first move to the city
from Down Home. I don't know what it is that she done.
But it make Mama make her family, whatever it was.
She live with us when I was little. I call her Naa Naa.
I remember when she move to the little house in Galloway.
The house have two rooms and a kitchen and it have a little porch.
And the gray shingles on her house look as old as she was.

She heish her gown over her head and she get dressed in the dark.
She run her hand over the few strands of hair she got left
then she tie a head wrap around it and put her straw hat on
to protect herself from the scorching heat of the burning sun
that she know is coming. She eat biscuits and molasses for her first
    meal.
Then she get the beans and cornbread in the tin can that she carry
    out to the fields
for her lunch. Pretty soon she know the cotton picking truck gone be
    coming.
She running late this morning. So she know she need to hurry.
It's already after 3 o'clock. She usually ready by now.
She put her hands on her back and she stretch herself out.
She gone be bent over all day. Her knees is already creaking.
She look over to the bed where Miz Irma is sleeping.
She wish she could lay back down. She think she must be getting old.
She set the wheelchair beside the bed for Miz Irma when she wake
    up

and she thank God that she got knees that's still able to creak.
"Thank you, Lord," she say, whispering under her breath,
"for health and strength that you give me. For two hands for to
    work."
If she lay her troubles beside another, she always pick hers back up.

She pull her stockings on and tie a knot at the knees.
Then she put on her brogans, run over at the heels.
She go sit out on the porch while she wait for the cotton truck to
    come.
In the sky, she look for the first tinge of the sun.
But the sun is still sleeping. Ain't got no need to come up yet.
Ain't nothing out this early but colored folks and the white
folks who carry them to work. The sun come up when it please.
She ain't never in her life done woke up with such ease
as the sun rise in the morning. She think about that song that say,
'that lucky old sun that ain't got nothing to do 'cept roll around
    heaven all day.'
She flex her arthritic hands and rub the rheumatiz in her knees.
Then she get her cotton sack from behind the old boards where she
    keep it.
Work is the only thing that she done ever knowed.
And, if she lucky, she gone work 'til the day she dead and gone.
Heaven, to her, is a place to go rest.
She want to see her mama too. She ain't never knowed her daddy.
Some white men kill him when she still a lap baby.
She go to work when she three to help put food on the table.
That's when she first start chopping cotton. Her mama make her a
    little hoe.
And she done worked ever since. Work is all that she know.

The cotton truck drive up and she get up off the porch.
She pull herself in the back and she say hello
to the other colored women in the truck. Clara, Nootie, and Sarah.
It's mostly men on the truck, too many to mention.
All told, it's bout 20 or 30 folks in the back.
The white man driving the truck name of Old Mr. Jack.
"How Miz Irma this morning?" Nootie and Clara both ask.

"She feeling kinda po'ly. Didn't sleep worth a damn."
"I made some root tea for her. Make show she drink it tonite."
And Nootie hand her a jar in a brown paper sack.
"Thank you kindly," Naa Naa say. "How y'all doing this morning?"
Nootie say, "Clara almost couldn't get away from her husband."
"Hush yo' nasty mouth," Miz Clara she say
"Ain't nothing wrong with yo' husband wanting to have his way…"

Both them women is crazy. They got her laughing from the start.
It make it easier to work when you got a smile in your heart.
That's what her mama always tell her. And she done learned it's the
    truth.
If working is yo' life, seem like it's better if you
find the goodness in it. Even in the worst of times,
she can find something in the day that is fit to make her smile.
She ain't never understood them people who complain and carry on.
You do what you gotta in life. You just do it and go on
with yo' head held high. With a song in your breast.
Going in and out the rows, her song seem to carry
her on thru the day. Even when her back is breaking.
Even when the strap on the cotton sack she hauling is weighing
more than she do. She always pick more than 500 pounds.
She a little bitty woman. No bigger than a 10-year-old child.
She fly thru the rows which is longer than a mile.
Her hands flying thru the bolls, sweat falling in her eyes.

She wipe the sweat off her brow with the kerchief round her neck.
She pick her first 100 lbs before the sun even up.
By the time the sun hang straight up in the sky,
she'll be near 300 lbs and so tired she almost crying.
Some folks try to trick the scales. They put dirt and rocks in they
    sack.
But she proud that she always do a honest day's work.

She gone be out there all day. Till near bout 5:00.
That's when she pass on the highway that run in front of our house.
I wait in the yard for the truck to come by.
She throw some money at me in a hankerchief tied

in a knot. I pick up the hankerchief off the ground.
I jump up and down when I see her bright smile.
I wave my hands and I call out, "I love you, Naa Naa. Thank you very
    much!"
Her lips mouth the words, "You so welcome, my baby."
I can't hear no sound but I know what she saying.
We been doing this ritual for years and years already.
I turn and go in the house, the coins in the hankerchief jingling.
She settle back in the seat, the paper sack in her lap.
She done caused joy in this day. And that make it all
worth it.

An excerpt of "Naa Naa" was first published in Raising Lily Ledbetter:
    Women Poets Occupy the Workplace by Lost Horse Press.

Annual reading at Elliott Bay Book Co. 2015

Brenda Wright

Margaret Barrie

Minnie Collins

Michael Hureaux

MARGARET S. BARRIE was raised in the Central District of Seattle in a loving village with family, neighbors, and friends. She's been a member of the African-American Writers' Alliance since 2012 and serves as treasurer. She participated in two anthologies published in 2018: AAWA's *Voices That Matter* and Renton Writers Workshop's *Spotlights*. She has read at the Seattle Public libraries, Elliott Bay Book Company, and the Highline Heritage Museum. She's presented descriptive works of poems that highlight the visual arts created by the painters and illustrators of the Onyx Fine Arts Collective and the Seattle Art Museum). She is a decade-long volunteer at the Seattle Public Library and lives with her husband Don Barrie in what was an ancient rainforest. She can be contacted at msbarrie@fastmail.com. She's also featured on AAWA's website author, and blog sections at aawa-seattle.org

A Glimpse of the Universe

On a cold and clear winter's morning
Seated in my kitchen, I look toward the horizon
Silver stars and a golden moon
Shine on a backdrop of cobalt blue
My spaceship, Mother Earth,
Spins toward bright
Splashes of light
Light after night after night
Like puddles of water
Yet in the sky
Near the shimmer
Bubbles of gas
Glow
Oh, the colors
Brilliant ruby red and carnelian orange
Gleaming viridian green and
The bluest lapis lazuli
stroke the sky
A glimpse of the universe
Embracing dawn
As our beloved
Gaia
Tilts toward Sun

"Ekphrasis" is defined as a descriptive work of prose or poetry that highlights the visual arts, in this case, paintings and drawings exhibited at the Onyx Art Gallery in downtown Seattle. The African-American Writers' Alliance was invited to respond to the works of the artists in the gallery. I selected four paintings and composed words evoked by my feelings and perceptions of the artwork, and I added the titles of the paintings to the poems. On August 25, 2019, I read to the artists and guests in the room.

Anywhere Cityscape
(Acrylic on canvas by Ashby Reed)

Some claimed
Insects
Took over
Others claimed
Humans
Took over
Overpopulated
Over built
Over consumed
All we have left are cityscapes
No landscapes
Pesticides from Monsanto
Wheat poisoned
Now
We eat
Gluten free
Prescription drugs
Oil spills
Polluted water
The list goes on
Fossil fuels
Cell phones
Microwaves
Cityscapes took the landscape
Carbon dioxide
Red orange skies
Before Gaia tilts toward the sun

Autumn Birch
(Acrylic on canvas by James Wilson)

Dust
Before mother earth
Tilts away from sun
Eyes of late

Winter Birch
(Acrylic on canvas by James Wilson)

Dawn
Blue horizon
Bright snow
Low light in sky
Eyes of new birth

Essence
(Mixed media by Earline Alston)

Young birch trees
swaying in breeze
Fresh water flowing down
Curving streams
Blossoms of magenta bright
Backdrop of pillowy clouds
Lush green flora
Sprout
Essence of Paradise
Essence of Paradise
Essence of Paradise
After humans are
Extinct

A Life Ending

Once upon four-years-and-hope, she battled cancer with the wish she would survive. She summoned her cousins to a meeting. She told them she wanted a celebration of her life, a living memorial before she passed, and she showed them the history of her illness, and then she let them know she had only a few months or less to live.

The cousins thought they were there to console her, but it was she who calmed and braced them, and the cousins told auntie the elder. Auntie, stressed by the urgency and aware of a life-ending, walked, dreamlike, the familiar path birds singing between the tall weeping trees while she continued strolling down the trail, through the ravine, between the steep hills, to be consoled by mother tree. Auntie knew she needed to see her soon and traveled to her. Auntie sat with her, and she allowed auntie to slowly, softly, and gently touch her hand, arm, and her essence. She looked ashen, her skin burnt by the treatments. They sat, Auntie listened. She reflected on her life and talked about her mother, Auntie's sister, who died of cancer years earlier. She said, "I wasn't really there for her."

Her children were always there for her, and much loved. She died that summer—forty-eight years young.

Auntie's distressed for her young adults
Who are still in need of a mother's love and care
Not sure when Auntie will realize she's not there

Auntie shares a poem written by the cousins.

> *Gonna miss our 'Lava Monster'*
> *We called her that when we were 'lil' and*
> *She would chase us everywhere*
> *We're sad for us, our family, and friends*
> *But she wants it to be a celebration*
> *If you really knew her*
> *You know how she rolled*
> *That smile and spirit was untouchable.*

True Love

Night before
He poured water into
Plug-in vessel
Dropped leaves in teapot

Next morning
She flipped switch
Heated the water
Set cups for two

The Fall

On an equinox Saturday
Earth tilted toward dawn
Reveals the sun
Our young neighbor came by
Wanted to clean
Side of our house
A week before
His dad pressure-washed
Their horizontal wall
Dirt and soap
Sprayed our wall
Like hard Styrofoam beads
Hence
He ran to grab a ladder
Set it up
Above lopsided cement stairs
He climbed the uneven ladder
Power washer in hand
Turned it on
Blew himself off
Down the stairs screaming
He was lucky he didn't break a bone

He fell
    On the
        First day
            Of Fall
                It was a fall
                    Not the Fall
                        Fall came but not
                            As expected!

Reading at Third Place Books in Seward Park

Merrie Ann Osborne, Minnie Collins, Helen Collier, Margaret Barrie, Georgia S. McDade, Jaye Ware

HELEN J. COLLIER, the twin of a deceased well-known Seattle attorney, is a native of Illinois. Writing has been in her spirit since her mother placed a pencil in her left hand and told her, "God made you a left-handed writer for a reason. It's up to you to share with the world what that reason is." Writing is a passion she developed early in her life and has always been a part of what she loves best. The prolific writer is best known for her favorite genre, sci-fi. Her books include short stories entitled *Looking for Trouble* which she published under the name Meow the Louisiana Catfish; *My Oprah in Remembering the Legacy*; a trilogy entitled *Ms. Anna and The Tears from The Healing Tree*, *The Two Worlds of Ms. Anna*, and *Ms. Anna The Promise Keeper*. Her latest novels are *The Unexpected* and *The Unexpected II: 2020 The Year When the Face of America Changed*.

In 1984 Collier relocated to Seattle where, for twenty-six years, she worked with incarcerated youth in King County.

She has been a proud member of AAWA since 1997. Check out Helen Collier's webpage: www.helencolliermeow.com

You are welcome to come sit with me, but remember it's my parlor we're seated in.

Willie the Blacksmith
A One-Act Play

Setting: 1940's Louisiana
Characters:
- **Willie**: Negro, blacksmith, 35-40 years old, tall, broad-shouldered
- **Customer One**: White male, 70 years old, wears a suit, and a white cowboy hat.
- **Customer Two**: White male, 35-40 years old, wears overalls, an apron, and a white cowboy hat.
- **Lillie**: Negro woman, 26 years old, dresses nicely.
- **Lester**: Lillie's husband, Negro, 35-40 years old, clean-shaven, wears a suit and tie, medium height, slender built
- **Mailman**: Negro, 60 years old, wears a mailman's uniform and hat, carries a mail bag.

Act 1
Scene 1

A blacksmith stands in his shop wearing thick black gloves, a leather apron with head gear covering his face. He pounds on a piece of hot metal while flames from a pit flicker in front of him.

A White man enters his blacksmith shop wearing a suit and a white hat.

Customer One: I want my hoss shoed.

Blacksmith: Dat's be five dollars

Customer One: I ain't paying no nigger five dollars to shod my hoss.

Blacksmith: Thare's a blacksmith up in Redbud shoe hosses. Ya best go see 'm.

Customer One: Dat's forty miles up the road or better.

The blacksmith continued to hammer.

Customer One: Dat Cracker wants ten dollars to shoe a hoss.

Getting no response, Customer One reaches into his pocket and pulls out a five-dollar bill and throws it on the floor.

Blacksmith: Redbud is de best place to go. Ya git de best service there I'm thanking. Ya can give da White man his money in his hand.

The blacksmith pounds harder on the hot metal, never giving Customer One any eye contact. Slowly Customer One takes a deep breath, cusses, picks up the money, and hands it to the blacksmith. The blacksmith takes off one glove, takes the money but never says a word.

Act 1
Scene 2

Customer One turns and walks out when Customer Two enters the blacksmith shop.

Customer One: If ya coming to git your hoss shoed it's gonna cost ya five dollars boy.

Customer Two grabs his hat from his head.

Customer Two: Ya know I ain't going to pay no nigger five dollars to shoe my hoss.

Customer One: Ya, is less ya wanta ride all the way to Redbud and pay ten dollars.

Customer Two: Say, let me have four dollars 'til I get back to the store. Give it back to ya then.

Customer One: Don't let that money hit the floor; that uppity nigger won't touch it.

Customer Two: Better be glad he's the only blacksmith in town or we'd have the Klan hang him.

Customer One: Nigger gitting besides hisself, but I ain't aiming to have no trouble out of Ida. Ya know what happened when the Klan killed her ole man.

Customer Two: Dat black witch must've called on three tornadoes back-to-back to come through the night of the hanging, nearly tore up the town.

Customer One: Them dat done the killing died before the last one come through.

Customer Two looked at the money in his hand, shook his head, walked in, and handed Willie his five dollars.

Act 1
Scene 3

A young lady walks into the blacksmith shop carrying a covered dish. Her skin has been lightened by some white man's seed. She smiles at the blacksmith. He smiles back, quickly pulling up a chair for her.

Blacksmith: Is this my Lillie I'm pleasured to see branging me some of her good cookin'?

He takes a seat beside her. She turns to him and hands him the covered dish.

Lillie: Willie, I'm mighty proud to hear you say that. And so that you know, Lester Ross has asked me for my hand in marriage. I think two years is long enough to wait for a man to propose to you. Wouldn't you say so?

The blacksmith lays the dish on the table. He stands up, shaking his head as he looks down at her. A frown covers his face.

Blacksmith: Why Lillie if I was to marry ya, I'd have to worry night and day trying to figure out how to protect ya and me, not to mantion our babies we'd have.

Lillie stands up, a disturbing look on her face.

Lillie: Why, Willie, ya big as any man 'round hare and just as strong being a blacksmith and all. I do believe ya're toying with my affections.

Lillie looks down at the dish of food, shakes her head, and walks out of the door.

Act 1
Scene 4

Two Years Later.

The blacksmith stands, hammering hot metal in his shop. In walks a man and a woman carrying a baby in a blanket. He stops and rushes over, dusting off two chairs for them to sit in.

Blacksmith: Lillie, Lester, what brangs ya two in hare in the middle de day. I sho' want a peep at dat little godson of mine.

Lillie sits crying, with the blanket covering her face. Willie stares at them. Lester takes a deep breath as he looks around, as if to make sure no one else is inside. He then slowly takes a seat in the chair offered him.

Lester: Late one night about a month ago after Lester, Jr., turned three months old, Lillie and I woke up hearing a banging at our front door. I hurried to see who it was.

Lester stops talking, gets up and looks out the door both ways, closes the door and locks it. He comes back in and retakes his seat.

Blacksmith: What is the matter? Has something happened?

Lester: Twelve o'clock one night Sheriff Hatman was knocking at our front door talkin' 'bout I needed to get out to my barn cause my cows done got loose. I jumped in my pants and run out to the barn looking all over the place. I shook my head wondering what he was talking 'bout 'cause not one of my cows was out runnin' loose. I turned to ask him what he was talking about but realized he had stayed in the house.

Lester shakes his head as tears roll down his face.

Lester: That dirty bastard was in my bed having Lillie while she lay there crying. Lester, Jr., was in his crib crying. When I went to grab him, he grabbed his gun he had laying there beside him on the bed and put it to Lillie's head. Kept right on doing his business 'til he got done. Afterwards he got up and told me if I want Lester, Jr., to live to be a grown man, I better let him in every time he come and he planned for it to be often. Said he didn't mind sharing Lillie with me. He'd been looking to have her a long time, and he planned to keep on having her now that he had a nigger to father any babies she had. Bastard been coming four, five times a week for 'bout a month. Lillie is a broken woman these days. She feels bad ,and I can't protect her cause of what might happen to little Lester, Jr.

Willie takes his hammer and begins beating the hot steel while Lillie sits crying.

Blacksmith: Lester, you take Lillie over to the house and wait for me thare. Momma's thare. I'll be on directly.

Lester rises, taking Lillie by her arm. She never looks at Willie as Lester leads her out of the shop. She continues to cry while holding her baby.

Act 1
Scene 5

It's a hot day. Willie is just finishing his lunch and is about to continue working when the mailman walks into his shop. Willie takes the letter the mailman offers him.

Mailman: Willie, man did you hear 'bout what happened to that dirty lowdown sheriff?

The mailman takes a seat. He doesn't wait for Willie to answer as he lowers his voice.

I heard it said that some White folks found him wandering around up town naked as a jaybird talking to himself. They had to take him down to Huntersville to that crazy house. No one seems to know what caused him to go crazy like that. Some of us glad though, many of our people he has sent to the pen for nothing.

Blacksmith: He's the big sheriff in town, hell on colored folks I reckon.

Mailman: Glad he gone, sorry he stayed so long. Good riddance.

He stands up, wiping his head; a smile lights his face as he walks out of Willie's shop.

Act 1
Scene 6

Willie closes the door to his shop, takes a seat, opens the letter the mailman has given him, and begins to read.

Lester: Hey, Willie man, I sho' want ya to thank your momma for that pouch she gave Lillie. It worked like a charm. When Sheriff Hatman came to the house that night Lillie and me lay waiting for him. Soon as he got naked, Lillie turned the lights off and let him crawl right in bed under the sheet with her. She opened that pouch and led his pole right inside of it. That cracker jumped up out of our bed like a streak of lightning had struck him. We heard him hollering loud as a bear as he run down the road, couldn't see nothing in the dark but his naked white ass. Left his gun and clothes right thare next to the bed. He didn't come back neither.

I decided to sell the farm. Got us a better place up hare in Mobile. I didn't understand what you meant when you told me it was too hard trying to protect a family down hare where the law don't work for us. Told me that right 'fore Lillie and me got married. Now that I realize what you meant I think I'll be raising my son to understand what you were trying to tell me. Me and Lillie thank you for sending us to your momma. She was truly the savior for us.

Willie rises and tosses the letter into the hot flames, watching it as it turns to gray smoke. He then puts on his face mask, apron, and gloves, and begins again to pound the hot steel.

The curtain closes.

A Letter from the Past: Klan Race Riots

There were no warnings that they were coming

Millions of stars filled the night sky.

Not a cloud in sight.

Nothing prepared us for their coming.

In the dead of night, their violence exploded.

Our lives were the target of their destruction.

Each way we turned, they defeated us.

They burned our homes.

They killed our babies, though we struggled to save them.

What could we do when there was no one willing to help us?

When their carnage was over, they left the dead behind.

Among the horrors, reminding us of their coming, was a torn white sheet hanging from the branch of a tree where death had taken its bounty.

Too Late

Rape was my bond long before I was born.

My black body stretched, pulled, and destroyed 'til it was void.

Ghosts haunt me now

Shadows lay at my feet.

From between my muddy legs, the babies came

all colors, shapes, and sizes

screaming, and dying as they bled in the land

by the slave master's hands

Like the boils on the body of 'ole Job,

I learned to separate the pains of my flesh from that of my

Soul.

God poured into me a supernatural endurance

As I said to myself

The slave master's vain lust is my insurance

I couldn't stop the sting of his whip on my hips

He couldn't stop the utterance of my lips

It's my mind you can't rape!

It's my soul you can't take!

I wept when they called it rape

For me, four hundred years too late!

Daybreak

In the dark of the night,
we wait for daybreak
With the coming of daybreak
We will see our lives
come together or become unglued.
Either way, the change will come
at daybreak.

Go Back to Africa

"Go back to Africa!" the white man screamed in my face as if to say this country belonged only to his race.

"I would go back," I said to him, "if I could only go alone, but I must take you with me."

"What do you mean take me with you?" he asked. "I'm already living in my country."

"All your genes and your DNA must go along with me as well as your white skin, you know."

"And what might I ask does that mean?" he asked.

"You cannot imagine how devastating it was for some of us when we discovered we were not White but Black. Our DNA from the man who caused our conception even our skin color indicated that we were White while the genes of our mothers said that we were not.

Yes, I would love to go back to the motherland, but I'm afraid you would have to come along. All those genes of yours you have given to us from the pleasures you enjoyed from using our Black female bodies from centuries back must come along as well and spill their deeds upon that land, which most likely would send us all to hell."

Excerpt from *Ms. Anna The Promise Keeper*

"You know, my love, it just kills me the way you are always talking about how the past should be buried and forgotten. Let's live in the present; right?" After dressing Raspy, Anna rushed around, getting ready for work. Raymond followed her with Raspy in his arms.

"It would help matters a lot, Anna."

"Let the dumb niggers forget the past while the white racist bastards build armies to annihilate us, I suppose."

"What damn army are you speaking of?" he asked, taking a seat on the bed while Raspy bounced up and down on his lap.

"What the hell do you call the Ku Klux Klansmen if they don't stem from the past?" Anna insisted, the smell of the burning cross Kenneth Mike had thrown in the stall where she worked still staining her nostrils. "When the Black Panthers sprang up across the country, the white power structure shot them down like dogs in the streets. But you know what they say when you tell them the Klan is still up in the hills building armies . . ."

"Oh, my God! Where is this coming from?"

"White men say that they know nothing of it, and those with the guts enough to admit it's true say there is nothing they can do to stop it. When all the time they know, it is their racist behavior they are protecting."

"That's bullshit! Something created in your mother's sick mind."

"It's bullshit, all right," she said, walking back into her bedroom.

"I love her. I swear I love her," Anna said aloud but to herself.

"You love her, but you would love her more if the man who fathered her had been a black man."

Annual reading at Elliott Bay Book Co. 2015

Santiago Vega

Alliniece Andino

Monique Franklin

Minnie Collins

Minnie A. Collins created Commemoration Plaques for Seattle's Historical Liberty Bank Building, authored books *The Purple Wash* and *Palm Power: Hearts in Harmony,* wrote the screenplay *Troubled Waters* with the Mahogany Project, and the essay "Sojourner Truth Prevails" for the National African American Clergy Women. Her works appear in *Raven Chronicles, WA Humanities Crosscurrents, Avocet, Blackpast.org,* and *Emerald Reflections-Seattle.* Her twelve-year membership in AAWA has been joyfully provocative.

Layered Lies

Lies lie layered in labyrinths of lore
Laid by legendary legions,
Lain since indigenous landscapes
Labeled "discovered."

Leveraged by his/her/their stories
Languished with arsenic
Leached and laced with lye, then
Legislated, legitimized into lethargic illogic
Of lopsided lascivious larceny
Lulling us into listlessness.

Enough! Enough! Lasso these lascivious leeches.
Expel their lionizing belles-lettres of lies!
Launching lucidity beyond layers of lies.

Revolutionary Dialogue

They say, Revolution is revolting;
I say, Revolution is positive.
They say, Revolution is destructive;
I say it's liberating, transformative.

Let me explain:
Revolution spins, unfolds minds,
Works out kinks and knots
Entangled in judgements, perceptions
Revolution: an endemic against inequities,
Testing attitude, heart, soul
Positive or negative for
Immunity from fear, isms, phobias
Because "we are not
In this together!
In solidarity, Revolution transforms.

Troubled Waters

Clothes, pots, pans, spilling out of crammed repurposed boxes, teetered across plywood floorboards. We were too weary, and I was ready for bed but had to fix something to eat. After years of renting and moving, we found finally something we, on two salaries, could handle monthly. This "something" the saleslady called a fixer-upper. She said that it would be a fun project for a young family. We could grow into it. As I stepped over boxes looking at rooms on my way to the kitchenette, I heard my son.

"Mom, Mom it won't go down!" "It won't stop going around," my four-year-old yelled. "Hurry Mom! Are you coming?"

"Is that your son calling? Why don't you go see what he wants? He's calling you, not me; sounds like he needs help."

"Don't you hear him?" I mumbled to myself. Plopping the dishcloth into the kitchen sink, I wiped my hands on my housedress, stuck my bare feet into my slippers and flopped down the squeaking hallway plywood floors. "I'm on my way," I consoled him.

As I opened the door, he grinned and pointed to a wad of tissue swirling in the deodorized toilet bowl. I smiled at my little man, too. Tangled ankle deep in his underpants, Tough Skin jeans and elastic Chadwick belt. I didn't know whether to scold him for pulling off too much tissue, trying to wipe himself, or to blame myself for saying "Yes" to his thirsty pleas for a second glass of grape juice for breakfast.

Laughter waned as I looked at the swirling water rising to the top of the bowl. I reached across my son's head and jiggled the toilet handle and elbowed him aside. "Watch out, it might spill over." "Pull up your pants."

"They won't come up. My belt buckle is twisted. Why won't the water go down? Stop it, Mom!"

Do I risk rising toilet water or untangle my son's pants and belt? I had to jiggle the handle. My eyes darted back and forth from his pants to the toilet bowl as I listened to the running and gushing toilet tank.

"Move out of the way now, while I try to fix it!" I lifted the heavy white ceramic tank top and slid it into the trash can beside the toilet. I looked inside a mucky stained tank and tried to remember how my dad stuck his hand many times into the water and squeezed the black ball to shut off the running water. "This shouldn't be too hard," I thought. My finger eased into the chilly rusty tank, careful to not get any crud under my fingernails: "I nudged the toilet ball and pulled the chain stopper. The darn thing gurgled, splashed, and squirted. The water rose to the top of the bowl, swirled, threatening to flood.

"Stay away," I grumbled. I plunged my hand into the toilet and pushed and pumped the toilet ball down until the water in the tank inched down. The toilet gulped its water and hissed at my attempts to control it. Afraid to flush the toilet, I closed the toilet seat top, put the trash can holding the tank top across the toilet seat and marched into the kitchen. My son, holding up his pants, scrambled at my heels.

Hunched over the kitchen table was my husband still buried in the morning paper, invoices, as he indulged in his third mug of caffeine. Without looking up, he mumbled, "What's going on back there?"

"That thing does not work! What did you do to it? It's going around and around. We can't use the bathroom," I shouted.

"Why not? It was working last night; what did you two do to it?"

"Well, last night is not today. It's not working! Can you fix it?"

"Ok, Ok, as soon I finish my coffee and deal with these bills."

I stuffed one fist into my housedress pocket, turned to the kitchen sink, and cooled my rising anger by slapping the dish cloth against the water, splashing water on myself and my son playing under my feet with his truck and airplanes. Slowly pushing the paper aside, my husband stretched his arm across to the nearby sink counter and dumped the cold coffee and grounds into the murky dishwater.

I wanted him to fix it now, repair this old toilet. I did not want to hear his usual, "I'll get to it this weekend" when he had time to go to the hardware store. I remembered how he told his buddies he was a "Do it yourself man." He spent hours in home stores talking to experts and collecting the right tools for home repairs. His tool belt grew to a tool box and was now boxed somewhere in the pile or in the basement.

I heard him trudge up the creaking basement steps as tools clinked and banged against the plaster walls. Then the clunk of the ceramic toilet tank, followed by jangles and jiggles of the toilet handle. "Get the mop! Can you at least do that right? It's everywhere!" He hollered. I dashed to the bathroom where water splashed, hissed, then gushed.

My son squealed, "What's wrong? What's he doing to the water?"

There my husband sat straddled across the toilet seat. Water trickled down his arms, elbows, knees and dripped on his running shoes. I wanted to laugh but cowered. "Do you need any help? Here's the mop." He shrugged his shoulders, "Maybe. Give me that box on the floor." I picked it up and read," Emporium Hardware Toilet Ball and Stopper – One Size fits All."

"When did you get this.? How do you know it will work? Do you think it will fit our toilet? This ball is white Styrofoam. Our ball is black and rubber. Our toilet is ancient. Let's call the plumber."

"For God's sake, will you just let me try it? Go do something useful in the kitchen."

Rebuffed, I slid the empty box onto the laminated sink counter, took my son's hand and guided him down the hall to be near me in the kitchen. An hour later after finishing my dishes, my son and I sheepishly tip toed to the bathroom. I stood at the doorway. Without stepping in, I asked, "Is everything okay?"

He knotted his brow. "No." He mumbled. "I never have the right tools, and you two are always breaking something. I don't know if I can handle all of this."

My body prickled as I heard the edge in his voice that meant to leave him alone. "Let me know what I can do…"

"I want you two to learn how to flush it right. If you don't, you'll be sent to the basement toilet that has no seat."

For the rest of the day, I cautioned my son to let me know when he had to go and reminded myself to stay away from that hissing that could spill over into deeper trouble.

NONI ERVIN has been an AAWA Member since 2019. As a young student, she found success in writing. The enjoyment of writing began in adulthood, and her first publication, *Verbatim: Living, Loving, Surviving*, was born, necessary because everyone has a story to tell. She has committed her actions in life to speak up for those who cannot speak up for themselves. This passion is how the *Kinara Park Kids* mini-series was created, including positive images of young Black/African-American children by incorporating the principles of Kwanzaa.

She admonishes, "Write daily."

Celebrating You

Today we celebrate you on your 90th birthday
Wow, so many things you have seen and experienced
So much love you have given and shared
So many hugs (in person and over the phone)
Your love for us has been like a winter coat that we are always grateful to have.

Today we celebrate you.
Knowing that you were praying for us.
So glad someone was praying with us.
Phone calls with you or a quick stop by the house
The comforting tone of your voice brings us back-to-center.

Today we celebrate you
In-the-know on just about every current event
Looking out for your loved ones
Cautioning and counseling us
You are endeared to so many.

We smile when we remember visiting you in Texas,
Or one of your many trips to Ohio, Oklahoma, Mississippi,
On your last trip to Seattle, we drove you up to the mountains--
Still snow on the ground in the middle of summer.
It was a quick snowball fight, and you, the uncontested victor!

You are fabulously wonderful--a beautiful woman
A dearly-loved mother, grandmother, great-grandmother
A beloved sister, cousin, aunt
A cherished friend and neighbor.
Be it church, a party, or any special event
You have the perfect hat for any occasion
Cobalt blue, shimmering pink
Bows and rhinestones adorn them all
Always fashionable and stylish
Big Mama, you are one Bad Chick!

Gratitude Freestyle

I am thankful for my family and friends
Those close or far away
Those here in body and those here in spirit
Love you

I am thankful for my dreams and goals
They keep me focused and steady
They remind me of those who have come before me
They inspire me to push through

I am thankful for you
Whether we agree or not
You help me find my voice
You make me better

I am thankful for gratitude
Appreciation, obligation, recognition
Today and tomorrow
For one more step, one more hug, one more kiss
I am grateful.

Lifelong Friends

They talked every day
Two, three, four times a day
About nothing and about everything
Whatever was on their minds

And boy did they laugh
Sometimes at each other
As they discussed life, love, and everything in between
They talked each other into some crazy things

Friday nights was their time to play
Dinner first: shrimp for one and anything for the other
We knew we could find them at any one of two restaurants
Adventurous and predictable
Great friends

Then turn the music up--turn it up loud!
They'd be dancing and jammin' all night
Otis Redding, Tyrone Davis, oldies and goodies
Their music from their time--smooth like merlot

They were educators and principals together
Twenty plus years side-by-side
They watched each other's children grow
Then graduate high school and college...
They celebrated the first grandchild on the scene

They talked every day
Two, three, four times, all-day
About nothing and about everything
Whatever was on their minds.

Cannonballs
(Inspired by Jacob Lawrence's painting Victory and Defeat, Panel 13)

I counted them all
22 Black cannonballs tell a story about the American struggle
They look like the heads of my enslaved African ancestors
On their way to the Americas in a ship packed so tight that surely death would be better
Moving across the Atlantic
Hoping to survive another tossing of the waves
And that smell... What is that smell?

Cannonballs as instruments of bloodshed and war
I see 22 polished Black women concubines used to grow the Deep South
Like cannons birthing Black babies
One after another
So there can be victory
Industry abounding
Buying and selling Black men, Black women, Black children... Industry abounding

There are 22 cannonballs that remind me of 22 Black women marching for women's suffrage
Still walking in the back...Still
Cannonballs like Black lives on the ground
Covered up by agendas and smoke and mirrors and deals that happen on the phone and never on paper
Monopolies and defense contracts, and
Let's go to war!

Cannonballs resulting in settlement and agreement
Every BODY giving up something
Mutually winning when losing and losing when winning
Shaking hands and tasting sweet victory
Reconciling our real cost and
Living with the lingering bitter aftertaste of defeat

Jacob Lawrence would say that the exchange is superficial and the sword is real
The colors are true
The angles are sharp
And the lines are without fault
Cannonballs representing a means to an end
Used to push over and move over and through obstacles
Used as a weapons to force victory

It is the polished Black cannonballs that remind me of
Our American struggle
22 Black lives
Reloaded into generational cannons
22 Means to an end

Rest in Peace
(Inspired by Jacob Lawrence's painting Peace, Panel 26)

Now, I said I wanted that section picked up
And that meant that whole section
Even over there next to that dry, cracked ground
I don't know how all those flowers grow there
You gotta be real gentle around the ones that are still growing'
And pull away any of the shrubs
Anything that might tangle up
Yellow ones, blue ones, green and red ones
It almost looks like the dead flowers have bloomed
I told them to clean that area up

I want it to look nice
The family is on their way and I usually give the red ones to the
      mamas
I save one blue one for their daddys
The rest of the people get whateva's left
It's real sad--happenin' too often
And the flowers aren't growin' back fast enough

When the family gets together, I cain't hardly tell 'em apart
Dang near spitting images of each other
I sure would like to stop seein' 'em show up here
I try to image what they might could look like grown' old
And that's gettin' harder and harder

I listen at stories from when they was little
But they just keep showin' up younger and younger
He was just startin' to live his life
Barely even a young man
Just dyin' so young
It don't seem right

I watch the news
Talkin' 'bout the struggle of America
I tell 'em: Y'all 'supposed to know y'all history

Better learn it, 'cause it's gon' come 'round again
All these pretty flowers and such - always some dead ones
This part right here is real nice
This'll make a good restin' place--real nice
I put some red flowers and some green flowers
And yellow and blue

Oh, out here fixin' up this plot
I done gone and lost track 'a time
The preacher will be here any minute
He always gives a nice eulogy.

MIZ PORTIONTÉ FLOES is a vocalist, author, producer, playwright, actress, and spoken word artist. While she cherishes many fond childhood memories, such as the Friday fish fry at her aunt's home and listening to music on summer nights with Granny Bea, Miz was no stranger to poverty or the byproducts that can impact families. She was surrounded by violence and poverty daily and had the misfortune of being witness to, and victim of, violence and crime.

The literary arts saved Miz. Through poetry she located an escape from the madness that surrounded her. As a woman, mother, grandmother, Miz Floes uses her past experiences to build and heal. She transforms pain into art and productively returns her art to the community!

Miz relocated to the Pacific Northwest from Illinois in 1991 and has been a member of AAWA since 2008. She is also a member of the Griot Party. Both critics and writers have described her sound as mature and steady with smooth lyrics. Her style of writing is refreshing, informative, intellectual, funny, and, at times, even sensual. Following *I'm Still Growing Vol. 1*, in 2005, she published *I'm Still Growing Vol. 2*, *Kweendom*, *Soulful X.Pressionz*, *Da 3rd Hour*, *Pearly Gates Jam Session*, *Royalty*, *I Ain't in Your Shadow*, *Jazzy Bluez All Up in My Soul*, and *4 Jazzy Soulz*. Her latest endeavor, *Poemz from the Pen*, features works from persons incarcerated in Washington State penitentiaries.

Red White & Black!

strange be the fruit dangling from the sycamore tree
unfortunately not so strange to see Mr. Wilson
wearing that white bedsheet
using the matching pillow case
a futile attempt to disguise his face
the older Black folk say the Klan is a White man's plan
to eliminate those of my race
too long we the Black have suffered injustices
a nation repeatedly disgraced
and yet they demanded my Black breast milk each day for
mine be that sweet black milk of the in-house slave
they viewed me through eyes of disgust and spoke to my strong ears
    in such bitter tones
how could those same eyes, view this same woman's milk fit
    nourishment for their babes
we the Black folk done cooked meals and cleaned those White folk
    kitchen
'twas our given task and daily mission
yet our presence was frowned upon, we ain't offered no seat at the
    dinner table
dirty, dim-witted and lazy; that's what the White folk here in
    America done labeled me and my kinsmen
Today White society would have me defend these inaccurate labels
    as common place
during the time it was legal for those of my race to be slapped in the
    face
simply because another felt disrespected
my ancestors were not protected, any thoughts of them having
    rights… quickly rejected
well long gone are those days
can't burn that cross on my lawn without consequence
today the Black American, is utilizing the right of self-defense
we were born on this soil
Yes it was our African and Indigenous ancestors that cultivated this
    land
Yet we are American!

it has slipped your mind... there once was a time
it was only my African ancestor, the plow, and the harrow for every
    row of your White cotton
it is quite clear that you've forgotten
my Black ancestors picked with mass toil and strife
to make cotton the fabric of your life
ipso facto... it was also my ancestors that strung the tobacco for the
    White man's dip snuff and chew
all due to our swollen Black and blistered fingertips
still we struggle to understand... why we must fight so hard for the
    title American
long before greed inspired a man to discover this
already occupied land
where the Red man would stand
before the White man's requirement of certifications and degrees
medications were prescribed
by the shaman of my ancestor's tribes
Black and Red nursing the White to the position of upright,
    performing surgeries without hospitals
Many groups have been formed over the years
to separate ... to eradicate
both the Red and Black race
take note... I not only fought for
but won my right to vote
I'm paying taxes for the parcel of land I own
I am Black as well as American
because America is my home
still I am mistreated and that's just not right
Show my people some respect... get your knee off of my Black
    brother's neck!
I'm only showing pride during a protest, with my Black Power fist
remove these modern-day shackles from my wrists
many of our Black generations still healing from the emotional
    scarring
left behind from the burnings, the hangings, the feather & tarring
my Black ancestors traveling in slave ships across unknown waters
my Red ancestors still walking trails of tears after hundreds of years

let us not forget to interject, both cause and effect
cause:
to cultivate stolen land and help it grow
effect:
the Evolution of the American Indian and the Negro
the so-called minority have overcome many tough situations
while building this Nation
Black and Red lives subjected to biased systems of education
pulled apart by the White man's dogs, shot with bullets from the
    White Man's guns, stoned with their rocks
forced into slavery, heads shaved, languages changed, sold again
    and again to the White man via that damned auction block
ridiculous abuse, the roped noose, unspeakable misuse we have
    proven to withstand
we were born on this land, where we currently stand
our Black and Red Lives Matter
we are citizens of America
we are AMERICAN!

Blackness Interrupted

It's a story our community knows all too well
A story that's agonizing, yet necessary to tell
It's a story not a fairy tale or fable
It's the story of a topic… long tabled
This is the story of the village that forgot the child

Once upon a time there was a bright-eyed little girl with hopes and dreams;
Chasing those butterfly fantasies
This little umber-toned girl … always aspired to fly higher
Higher than those butterflies she chased
Until the day she experienced the taste of pain
She had flown into a cloud of crack cocaine
It rocked her world
She … her mother's 1st born
that bright-eyed baby girl
Now mommy's cheeks are always stained with tears
She can't help but … FEEL
Blackness interrupted: the dream has been deferred
A forgotten and yet worthy cause
Royalty has taken a pause
And suddenly it affects us all
Still this daughter is no burden
She is a gift
She was created to educate… to demonstrate
Greatness and pass the knowledge
But this young drug abuser
Took a wrong turn…
Still we as a people can't afford to lose her
With the birth of greatness
Comes great responsibility
This is no burden … quite the contrary…
The cause… still worthy
As addiction unfolds…
Her true purpose
Her true direction

Her BLACK life... is on hold
She's in her early 20's and yet her body FEELS
broken down and old
Feels like she's got a head or chest cold
Yet the rumors say Black folks are safe
and 19 is a conspiracy anyway
She continues to share that glass pipe with the other crack- heads
    she befriends
No thoughts of where they've been
Or who they were exposed to
She hasn't got a clue
Dee and Jesse look clean
I mean it didn't matter in that moment of crave
Ain't nobody gonna catch **Corona** anyway
She takes another hit
As her neighbor, I can't help but to FEEL
Blackness has been interrupted, her dreams... deferred
Still her life is a worthy cause; while only one Queen has taken a
    pause
As a community it effects, us all
Our beautiful daughter is lost
Her thoughts scattered, her dreams shattered, on Seattle's streets
    being battered
She has forgotten that her little Black Life Matters!
During her addiction loved ones have grown old and died.
Her ears have gone deaf to her mother's cries.
The pleas from her sister and brother ... mattered before
Not anymore
The butterfly chaser morphed into a fiend
chasing green and gotta make it by any means
In need of that temporary fix ... Still on the block turning tricks
Even after she got sick
Caught that 19
that COVID they said Black folks couldn't catch
She listened to the rumors while ignoring the facts
And a mother can't help but to FEEL
Self and family values descend
We FEEL sad within

That once bright-eyed baby girl
now seems lost to the world
Yesterday heard it from a trusted friend
her little sister is now sampling heroin
Come on, village
The children need us
it's all about the we
we've given birth to the community
this Black existence we must defend
The time has come for all who possess melanin
to transcend
this great Blackness can no longer be interrupted
Our dreams must make the transformation to reality
Our thoughts to fruition
Some have forgotten our worthy cause
Many have taken a pause
it has tremendously affected us all
We've forgotten … It takes a village, yawl!
The time has come to heal
Can you feel… me?

IT'S TIME TO GROW like a plant in the rain
GROWING like a child, looking for avenues to escape the pain of this world
I've grown to woman from girl

G-R-O-W
What does it mean to grow?
I don't know... I guess it differs from person to person

Greet
Reach
Observe
Wisely

Each time I think before I speak... I grow
Each time I make the conscious choice to utilize my voice and reserve my fists... I grow
When I exercise my ability to recognize ignorance, as an opportunity to teach... I grow
In these days of tragedy, darkness, and fear
I walk with caution and awareness
I observe all around me
I can see

That they've been very busy... strengthening their hateful army
The Klan, the Q, the so-called white supremacy
They've come together for their common cause

The other day
I observed, as they shouted USA!
and breached the Capitol Building
I watched, with tear-filled eyes at their attempt to make a mockery of this country

I searched my headspace for what was not seen.
On my television screen
The behind-the-scenes plan
the angle, the scheme

These hate groups feel that they are supreme
The mere thought of what's next
Brings my spirits down... my brow to a frown

We need to... G-R-O-W

Graciously
Reinvent
Our
World

My first thought...
I don't want to see another black body hit the ground
Due to the so-called law enforcement representatives of the town
Yet, before the thought could be processed
Another Black body struck...
I wanted to say... Kenosha what the?
For real?! another cop that will not stand trial for his crime
Another legal ear turned deaf, another judicial eye turned blind
While there is a continued effort to eliminate those of my kind

Not one dared to ignore what happed on January 6th in Washington, D. C.!
Now the powers that be can see
now they view these hate groups as a problem
now that they have threatened democracy
same groups weren't viewed as a serious problem
when they were choking, pepper balling, shooting, and killing those like me!
We need 2 Gro.
No more strange fruit!
Protect your family tree.
Preserve the bloodlines of yours and mine
We need to GROW...
- Closer as a Black community
- Our children up in love and awareness
- Our army and prepare for battle

There is a war on **Black**, we are under attack
There is a war on poor
Need I say more?

Get
Ready
Organize
Wisely

TRACI HARRELL is an international best-selling author and President of It's All Bigger Than Me Consulting, a full- service training, coaching, and transformation company specializing in Leadership, Inclusion, Diversity & Happiness for leaders, teams, and organizations. Traci is a certified Success Coach® through SUCCESS Magazine, and she is leading the 'Bigger Than Me - Success Series', a strategic initiative designed to foster inclusion and systemic change, while building a legacy for future generations. She has over 25 years of diverse Leadership experience in Corporate America with 8 years at IBM, 14 years at Disney, and 5 years at Microsoft. Traci offers a results - driven positive and joyful approach when addressing Diversity & Inclusion, using her new methodology called, Transformational Inclusive Leadership, with Mind, Heart & Soul. She invites each of us to lean into a new level of awareness, action, and accountability. Traci says, "Being IN, is the WIN, on the Journey to SUCCESS!"

Transformational Inclusive Leadership, with Mind, Heart & Soul
(The Bigger Than Me – Success Series)

Our Shared Problem: The ideals of Racial Justice, Equity and Inclusion that have fueled protests in the streets of America and around the world, should also be fueling conversations about Inclusion, Mental Health, and Safety 'inside' the workplace. The purpose of this essay is to add a new level of urgency to our actions, by spotlighting solutions for experiences that can be harmful and traumatic, which continue to happen as an embedded part of the business world, like Unconscious Bias, Similarity Bias, Unequal Performance Standards, and a lack of Leadership Accountability. Although most companies offer Diversity training to define some of these topics, many are not focusing on the full problem and are unsuccessful in addressing the real impact of these challenges on real people at work. The Good News is, we have solutions for these challenges.

From the boardroom to the mailroom, from Microsoft to McDonalds, from non-profits to academics, from corporate culture to the corner store, ALL organizations share a critical compound problem. We must address the urgent need to: 1) prioritize the importance of 'Inclusion for All' at a systemic level, 2) acknowledge the variable or different experiences that some employees often have in business and 3) simultaneously and intentionally focus on new strategies, new experiences, and new approaches to co-create new desired outcomes in the areas of Diversity, Equity, Inclusion, Justice and Belonging.

Exclusion is a daily experience for many - in particular, women, African Americans, those with disabilities, GLBTQ, and other marginalized groups have a long-documented history of being excluded. Decades of research exists about barriers to leadership and solutions exist also. Volumes of Academic journals and well-intentioned research studies abound, which summarize the 'Key Challenges' that many diverse workers experience in business as part of the current 'system'. Whether these are microaggressions, repeated experiences, or single devastating decisions, they can be abusive and traumatic.

The neuroscience of exclusion clearly equates these experiences of Inequity and Exclusion in the workplace with real pain, mental health concerns, physical harm, psychological distress, Anxiety, PTSD, lack of Trust, and many other negative outcomes.

As a result, the conversation around achieving Inclusion and stopping Exclusion, should rise to the top of the priority list for every executive, leader, and worker.

Now is the time for us to prioritize real systemic changes to ensure we eradicate the assault on Inclusion wherever it exists, with a new focus on what *really* happens inside all organizations.

My Journey – A Little Background & A No-Brainer: For nearly 3 decades, Diversity & Inclusion has been a serious passion of mine. Like many, I have always volunteered my time and energy, and took on extra roles in the companies that I worked for and in the Communities where I lived, to create a space for improvements. Then, over five years ago, prior to the country's current racial reckoning and rediscovery of our humanity, I felt an overwhelming responsibility to change the status quo.

A young girl's story of near suicide changed me.

I started leading a strategic initiative within Corporate America, called the *Adaptive Leadership Equity & Inclusion Initiative*™, which originated from a humble notion and a burning desire to create Inclusion, Equity, Justice and Safety, both immediately and for generations to come. I experienced professional trauma first-hand too. I have also documented thousands of interviews with real people on all-sides of the equation, and we have decades of research. I led local initiatives, and our National Think Tanks all shared the same results. What more did we need? Really? It was all a No-Brainer. I couldn't make sense of the lack of progress. It was easy to find leaders like myself in the business world who would 'say' the right things, but I was also a leader in my community, and we needed to see real actions and lasting change at a systemic level.

We then formalized the *Bigger Than Me - Success Series™* by bringing together hundreds of D&I Experts, Community Leaders, Inclusion Champions, engaged Allies, impacted Individuals, and WOKE™ Executives from various industries around the world. The process was both intentional and organic. Together, we moved from focusing on single D&I training 'events,' to amplifying our efforts as a strategic initiative...we created a 'movement.'

We shared an open invitation to join the *Bigger Than Me Movement™*, which is an opportunity to participate in Inclusion experiences, and to build community for real connections and deep transformations, as an individual, group or organization.

Our Call to Action: *Transformational Inclusive Leadership with Mind, Heart and Soul™* is a collective Call-to-Action to invite organizational leaders, workers and professionals around the world to immediately embrace a new level of urgency and ownership when considering how they approach Equity & Inclusion in business. This open invitation creates an opportunity to address racial unrest around the world, by embarking on a new journey to gain a deeper level of 'Awareness, Action & Accountability.'

Today, many business leaders are making grand declarations about hiring more diverse workers to 'Achieve Racial Equity & Inclusion.' These hiring efforts are "doomed to fail," without new strategies and priorities focused on *Inclusion & Belonging* at a systemic level, according to extensive research from Harvard University, the National Academy of Sciences, and the World Economic Forum. Decades of research shows that *the Business Case for Diversity is a "Failed Strategy",* according to recent articles in Fast Company, the New York Times, the Wall Street Journal, Harvard Business Review and more. It should be widely known that only business leaders that prioritize efforts to "build their *Inclusion* muscles will reap the benefits of Diversity." Additionally, only leaders who are willing to engage personally in deeper transformational experiences, will reach the goals of Inclusion and Belonging that are critical for change at any real systemic level. This is also directly linked to business and organizational success at all levels.

My Mission in Life: Despite all the existing facts, and the known challenges, the lived experience of many diverse professionals (who looked like me) still remained 'unchanged.' And just to be clear, the experiences are not 'the same,' in a good way – it was in a, "Are we really still having the same conversations after 50 years," kinda way.

I had to ask myself the same questions that we all should ask ourselves right now. If we don't step up to drive change NOW, who will? And when? These age-old questions glared directly into my heart...into my soul... and I knew I had to be an agent for change, a force for good, a resource to create a space for others to lead change also. My mission in life is clear...I am destined to leave a roadmap for Success. We can't just keep talking about change, we must align our words with our actions.

In addition to writing a series of books, and completing a series of video documentaries, my goal is to amplify the "Importance of Telling Our Stories." As Brené Brown says, "Stories we own, we get to write the ending, and stories we don't own, own us. We are helping participants in our Community Webinars and Inclusion Experiences, to tell their stories. My goals include helping participants in the process to see the importance of embarking on and embracing the Journey of Inclusion.

Our Approach to Change: The ultimate goal of the process called, *Transformational Inclusive Leadership, with Mind, Heart and Soul* is to master the concepts of Diversity, Equity, Inclusion & Belonging for ALL, so that businesses and organizations of all kinds, can fully reap the benefit from the Business Case for Diversity. The idea of "creating a safe and inclusive culture where all individuals and employees can thrive" is a stated goal of almost every business. We all desire Inclusion intuitively. Belonging is a North Star and a fundamental human need for safety.

There's more good news. We have some real answers. It's not the only way, but we have a clear roadmap for Success. This new concept of Transformational Inclusive Leadership builds upon and integrates: 1) proven research and relevant studies, 2) industry best practices, 3) ageless wisdom, 4) strategic programming, training, and consulting used within organizations, and 5) and collectively over a thousand years of real-world professional experience. Bottomline, it works.

For practical purposes, we have leveraged the 'Bigger Than Me – Success Series' by creating a series of community training events, panel discussions and leadership engagements, to establish a baseline for success with select leaders and organizations ready to embrace this journey. This will be both an individual and shared experience, where we have created a clear roadmap that any leader, team, or organization will be able to leverage, regardless of where they are on their Diversity & Inclusion journey.

As a starting point, "one powerful way to make the case for an inclusive culture is to look at the impact of exclusion." Extensive research, including studies by Naomi Eisenburger at UCLA found that "being excluded activates our pain system, suggesting that it is a threat to our very survival." Yes - the same receptors in our brain that process physical pain are activated when we experience exclusive practices in the workplace. *Any person concerned with the success of their organization can link the simple truths of this work with their own Success, for Urgency & Action.*

Participants of the *Bigger Than Me Success Series* have been eager to share the beginnings of their learnings.

> *"This year has been eye opening for me..." shared Erica Stricker, Managing Director at CBRE, supporting Microsoft globally. We could "say we're doing all the right things..." but "...the bigger problem is that I have a hole in the bucket issue where I've got a larger percentage and ratio of individuals that are diverse, both ethnic and racial, that are leaving the organization over those that are not...We might have thought that we had our things figured out... But guess what, we don't. There is a lot more work to be done... I'm excited for what the future will bring."*

Our journey to Ignite Inclusion for ALL requires the important step of identifying and addressing current inequities that exist everywhere, while lovingly creating a space for Leaders and Teams to learn and grow together, with a high-level of intention. We lead with love, peace & grace, with a focus on results.

Our Shared Solution: *Transformational Inclusive Leadership with Mind, Heart and Soul* is one of the many tools that we invite leaders to leverage to invoke new behaviors and outcomes in the areas of Diversity, Equity, and Inclusion. The *Bigger Than Me-Success Series* presents an opportunity for leaders and professionals, both individually and organizationally, to choose a new level of ownership and urgency - to first acknowledge that clear challenges exist, and then to join us on an intentional journey to drive positive change.

The foundational principles of *Transformational Inclusive Leadership with Mind, Heart and Soul* are built upon 4 key pillars of proven research which include: 1) Positive Psychology, 2) Adaptive Leadership, 3) Self-Directed Learning, and 4) an optimized practice that I call, 'Growth Mindset-in Action'. The systemic changes needed to create a Diverse and Inclusive culture where all employees can truly thrive requires new levels of awareness & engagement, deep personal & professional transformation, and individual & organizational accountability at all levels.

This strategic initiative is designed to transform leaders, individuals, and organizations by 'Growing the Mind, Opening the Heart, and Developing the Soul.' Embracing *Transformational Inclusive Leadership with Mind, Heart & Soul*™ offers practical solutions which include an iterative activation and implementation lifecycle with seven proven phases.

Now is the time for us to 'Rebuild Trust, Rethink Training, and Address Trauma - Together.'

We are creating *space* and offering *grace* while building an online community of leaders in training and in practice. Join us as we illuminate a pathway for deep introspection and new actions designed to transform lives, with a new SUCCESS-filled, results oriented approach to Diversity, Equity, Inclusion, Justice & Belonging.

Merrie Ann Osborne, Helen Collier, Jaye Ware, Margaret Barrie, Georgia S. McDade

GAIL HAYNES, poet and author of *Soulful and Sassy Reflections and Poems*, has graced many platforms throughout Seattle and King County with her fun and candid writings that sometime come with a sassy attitude.

Gail has been a member of AWAA since 2015. She creates poems that are soulful and sassy, poems that will make you laugh and also reflect on real-life experiences. Among the sites where she has read are Mount Zion Baptist Church, Elliott Bay Book Company, Columbia and Ballard Library, and Life Enrichment Bookstore. Gail shares her poems at non-profit organizations that stand against injustice. Many of her poems exalt the goodness of the Lord and His amazing power of love to transform lives. *Soulful and Sassy Reflections and Poems* is the author's first book. Her advice appears in The Facts in the column "Be Well with Gail."

Gail enjoys writing and gives God the glory for her gift.

Coming to Jesus Out of the Ditch

This was her day to rise up into her authentic self. She had been through much pain, disappointment and shame; she heard God's voice call out to her "Come to me my daughter so I can restore you from the damage and pain you've suffered." as she walked, she stumbled, and the heel of her designer shoe broke off, but God positioned angels on both sides to catch her before she fell.

As she emerged out of the ditch where she'd been, she felt the warmness of God's love shine on her tear-stained face. By this time her mascara had smeared, and her $3,000 weave was coming loose. Her story began less than one year ago when a man swept her off her feet. This man was not only drop-dead gorgeous but very rich.

She fell hard for him like white on rice. She was so sure this man was her God-given gift from Heaven above. She trusted and gave her life to him wholeheartedly; she didn't realize she was slowly descending into a ditch of passion, lust, and a deceptive love that couldn't satisfy. You see she was looking for love in all the wrong places. While standing at the wedding altar she looked around at all her friend's smiling faces and clapping hands screaming "Congratulations, girl." Through all the Girl Congratulations and smiles she assumed she'd be envied by women everywhere.

She licked her red lips as she flipped back her hair. Her long diamond studded eye lashes fluttered as she looked deeply into his eyes and said "I Do" while holding his hand. She whispered, "I'm so blessed God gave you to be my man." As he smiled and lightly kissed her cheek, she glanced around to see if anyone saw that kiss. He replied, "I do," and whispered, "Thank you, baby, I'm blessed to have you too."

Just like Eve who listened to the serpent and ate the fruit, she too was unknowingly deceived. It wasn't long before she was crying on her knees saying, "God, help me please" for the same smiling faces that said congratulations girl! were now the same ones who shamed her with a disgusted look on their faces saying, "Girl you knew he was no good; you are a disgrace." Only ten months later her gorgeous, rich husband ran off with another woman, a love story gone sour real fast.

One tear drop of grace and mercy came from the Lord who she rejected when He said to her, "This is not the man I sent you, my daughter." She didn't listen, for she believed all she needed was this man in her life, no one else not even God. As she cried out, God's unconditional love broke the soul-tie that connected her to this man. She soon became free to crawl, climb, and walk out the ditch of deception to victory. Wasted and stained was her beautiful white Versace designer wedding dress; her beautiful $3,000 weave was now a hot mess; the lonely diamond ring sat on her finger, her bouquet of flowers wilted and dying as she thought of her husband's cheating and lying. "Lord, forgive me for leaving you; I now know you are the one who really loved me"

As she came out of the ditch her footing became sure. God cleaned and washed her through and through, gave her a new purpose and life filled with joy. She thought maybe I needed to go in the ditch to realize that God's love is all I need. Experience and struggle can sometimes be the best teacher. As she rose into her authentic self, all the pride, glitz, and glamour were gone for good. She realized no one could bring her real love and peace but the Lord. She humbly walked with purpose, glad to be free, loving herself with the victory. She later pawned the diamond ring and Versace wedding dress at a high-end consignment shop and gave the money to her single-parent sister who she had not spoken to for many years because of her prideful, uppity attitude.

Annual reading at Elliot Bay Book Co. 2015

Gail Haynes

Alliniece Andino *Helen Collier*

LEOMA JAMES is a young poet, storyteller, activist, and educator from Seattle, Washington. She primarily writes poetry and short stories that focus on the Black experience, from a global standpoint. She is very energetic and has a passion for immersing herself in culture, language, and history. Leoma is a world traveler who studied at the United States International University through the Knowledge Exchange Institute in Nairobi, Kenya. That pivotal experience propelled her to serve in Namibia from 2017-2019 as a Secondary English teacher with the U.S Peace Corps. She is currently in the process of finalizing her first novel, *No Blame, No Shame, No Guilt* that discusses her profound experience as a Black American Woman living in Africa and examines white supremacy as a global issue through the form of short stories and poetry.

Leoma is currently pursuing her master's degree in Education at the University of Washington and has the desire to support students who are disadvantaged academically and socially due to race, socio-economic background, immigration status, and language or communication barriers.

Her submissions were inspired by the Onyx Fine Arts Collective and the Women of Wonder Art Gallery in Seattle. Both black-centered exhibits that honor and celebrate the creativity, resilience, and beauty of black people around the world.

Pacific Place

Melanated pictures hang on the walls of a building I thought they'd
	never be in.
The place where I couldn't afford to shop in.
The place where black bodies came for movies
and Johnny Rockets
and looked at jewelry through the window at Tiffany's
but kept walking.
We drank samples from Teavana
and rode escalators from top to bottom,
but now we come to embrace our talents
and celebrate the artists.
It's truly beautiful.
How life can come full circle but still leave you in a square.
It's amazing that we're represented
but I don't want you to shop here.
I don't want you to buy our black bodies
and hang them on your wall.
I don't want you to spend your dollars and think reparations are that
	small.

Your buying black art should not be the end all be all.
You support our dreams but still support our fall.

I went most of my life without seeing my face
Represented as beautiful or strong, as seen in this Place.
You are not threatened by these paintings
that hang on the wall
because they don't talk back, and they don't respond.
You are left to interpret the pain that you've caused.
You are left to examine the depths of our hearts.
The colors, the style, the stroke of each brush.
No wonder they're afraid when we embrace us.

Understood
(Inspired by the painting A Reversal of Fortune by Bonnie Hopper)

I think this woman knows me
I think she sees me
and understands some things I don't talk about
Some things in my core, some things I've forgotten about
Like childhood trauma that's
pushed to the back of your brain.
That's lost in the memories
so you don't feel the pain.

I think she knows me
She is a painting on a wall but somehow,
she's alive and knows my heart
She's strong and she's bold with superpowers
I could look at this painting and be mesmerized for hours.

She knows me and I know her even when names
aren't exchanged
She sees me unscathed but still knows my pain

I am so in awe of Black women
I could feel down and small but then a Black woman could come and
 change it all
Not only the one who birthed me
but the ones who birthed this earth
Because the truth of the matter is our ancestors were first

Thank you, Black women, for knowing my name
Thank you, Black women, for healing my pain
For listening to my heart, and hearing what I don't say.
For breaking your back and paving the way
For giving me a chance when others closed the door,
For giving me love and picking my heart off the floor.
I am honored every day to be a part of the crew
I love you, Black women, for all that you do.

Annual reading at Elliot Bay Book Co. 2015

Alliniece Andino

Minnie Collins

Gaylloyd Sissón

Georgia S. McDade

GEORGIA STEWART MCDADE joined AAWA the year of its founding, 1991. Georgia S. McDade's favorite description of herself comes from a former student: "You're not just a great teacher of literature—you teach sociology, anthropology, history, economics, political science, psychology, journalism, religion! And politics: I never thought of everything being political until I took your class." It's no surprise that she would write. Her books include *Travel Tips for Dream Trips*, four volumes of poetry called *Outside the Cave*, and a collection of stories, sketches, and essays entitled *Observations and Revelations*. She hopes to spend more time working on two biographies and a book on novelist Jessie Fauset.

With Jim Cantú, she co-hosts KVRU's "Hearts and Soul" and contributes to *South Seattle Emerald*. She also writes regularly for *Leschinews*. Occasionally, she reads her poetry, speaks on and teaches a variety of subjects including religion and Shakespeare.

The Greens
4/16/15

New growth green!
Old growth green!

Fern
Oak
Spruce
Elm
Alder
Pine
Crayola can't touch this!

Two for One
(2006, Inspired by Elizabeth Halfacre's collage Mom's House, Dad's House)

Two toothbrushes
Two deodorants
Two beds
Two alarm clocks
Two VCR's
Two Thanksgivings
She would have gladly relinquished one-half her
    belongings.
She would have settled for their loving each other one-half
    as much as each loved her.
She would have gladly given up Dad's one house and
    Mom's one house.
All she ever wanted was two parents in one house, a house
    neither Mom's house nor Dad's house but rather our house.

The Cranes
1/4/20

The cranes are coming!
The cranes are coming.
For three years Seattle has been the crane
    capital of the U. S.
Why be surprised the cranes are coming
    to your neighborhood?
Surely you did not think the cranes would stop downtown?
The cranes dig deep.
The cranes dig wide.
The cranes never build only.
The cranes always destroy first.
No more P-patch.
No more Red Apple.
Where is Mr. James Washington's sculpture?
Of course, people will marvel at the new
    creations.

But, at least for a while, some of us will
    cringe at the coming of the cranes and
    the destruction they bring.

What Raffles Wrought
2018

In 1985 I was at the desk of a Sims Guest House in Singapore inquiring about the iconic Raffles Hotel. I knew Hemingway and other writers had often gathered at the now nearly 100-year-old hotel, so, as a writer, I thought I should go there too! I learned the hotel was not very far, so I set out walking.

A man I had seen in the guesthouse more than once ran to catch me and said he would accompany me if I wished. I decided, despite my sister's warning not to speak to strangers, that he could come along. He stopped and said, "You need to know I can afford only the dessert." Glad to have some company, I said ok,

We introduced ourselves. Jed was his name. He told me he was from Australia, a writer, and had been to Raffles because famous writers often visited. We reached the hotel, got a table. I looked at the menu and said, "I too can only afford a dessert." Both of us laughed. We conversed about our travels, especially Singapore where he had visited several times. He usually wrote about cars in a magazine comparable to *Car and Driver*, but he wrote stories too. He loved Joseph Conrad, told me Conrad had visited Raffles. *Heart of Darkness* consumed much of our conversation. We also talked about my favorite Conrad story, "Youth." I told him about my trip around the world and answered questions he had about the trip. Because he knew Singapore well, he told me what I had to see. We had a really pleasant conversation.

When we returned to the guest house, we exchanged addresses. We waved at each other on a few occasions.

About two months later I returned to Seattle from my six-month trip around the world. I was exhausted in the best way. Among the mounds of mail was a letter from Jed—eight single-spaced pages on onion-skin paper. This was the beginning of a long epistolary adventure. Letters ranged from seven to seventeen pages. Many of his letters were about American history, history I had forgotten or never knew. I've forgotten why he first mentioned the *Monitor* and the *Merrimack*, but he mentioned that battle often. I finally had to check a history book before I could respond. He loved Civil War history and knew it well. I do not recall how he came to know my name is Georgia Lee Stewart McDade. But he decided that the "Lee" in my name was proof I am a descendant of Robert E. Lee! No amount of telling him that probably was not the case changed his mind, and he wrote my entire name on every letter he addressed to me. He talked about American elections. He mentioned his sister and how they were at odds. He told me more about his travels. He commented on my stories I often sent him for criticism—said he always recognized me and that should not be the case. He loved American television. References to the television show "In the Heat of the Night" abound. But his favorite show was "Law and Order." He must have mentioned it in every letter! I had never seen it, just hadn't gotten to watching it. He referred to it so much that I finally watched an episode and soon became a fan, still am! He loved American cars, so several years I sent him a calendar of cars.

 What bothered me in his letters were the racists comments about the Aborigines of Australia and the Japanese. He NEVER said anything positive about either group. I would write that he should not make such comments, tell him the Aborigines are people, were there long before he and his compatriots, had a right to the land. He always called the Japanese "Japs." I told him "Jap" was derogatory, that he should use the word "Japanese."

 He responded, "I know what you are saying, what you mean, but I know them; you don't." That would anger me more, but eventually I would answer. I'm sure I would have written far more often had he not included the rants and racist language

 We probably exchanged six or seven letters a year over a twenty-year span. In May of 2005 I received a letter from a barrister (lawyer) in Australia telling me that Jed had died and left me $10,000! I was amazed on two counts. I hadn't heard from him in a couple of months but had no idea he was ill. I ran back to get the latest letter I had received. It reads: "I'm so glad that someone as warm as you are in the world doing all the good you do. Don't let anyone change you." I finished reading the barrister's letter. He said the executor of the will was out of the country and would not return until September. I forgot about the letter.

 In early September I received a note and a check in the mail. I emailed the executor thanking him and asking what had happened to the fifty-five-year-old Jed. He said one day Jed came into his office wanting to have his will made. The two men had been in the military together, had not seen each other in over twenty years. Jed was coughing, said he did not know what was wrong with him. He wanted Georgia Lee Stewart McDade to have $10,000.

    I used the money to buy my first MAC laptop—stolen about five years later—and go on a fifteen-day tour of eight national parks. The woman most often my travel roommate during this trip was an Australian on her first trip to the United States.

NANA KIBIBI MONIÉ is Seattle-born and she has received several distinguished titles and honors. She's an Evergreen State College graduate with a BA in Communications; earned a MA from Seattle University in the Executive Master of nonprofit department and has earned a Certificate in cinematography from The New York Film Academy.

Presently, she is the Executive and Artistic Director of Nu Black Arts West Theatre, the oldest African-American Theater Company in the Pacific Northwest, 20+ years, Ms. Monié is the first African-American President of the American Federation of Television and Radio Artists (AFTRA) 1996-1999 for Washington, Oregon, Alaska, and Idaho.

This accomplished actress, singer, and playwright has written several one-act plays; and is the only woman that has directed August Wilson, the double Pulitzer Prize winner, in a reading of his play *The Homecoming* at A Contemporary Theatre in Seattle, Washington.

Nana Kibibi is a Nana (Queen Mother) in Ghana West Africa. She has also worked with many well-known celebrities: Stevie Wonder, Billy Preston, Guitar Shorty, Roy Ayres, Hank Crawford, opened for Gladys Knight and the Pips, The Dramatics, and many other well-known icons.

Ms. Monié was elected president of Seattle's SE Rotary Club 5030 in 2022. She is an active member of the National Council of Negro Women (NCNW), Sixth Regional Diaspora Caucus (SRDC), Association for the Study of Classical African Civilizations (ASCAC), and Screen Actors Guild/American Federation of Television and Radio Artists (formerly AFTRA, now SAG/AFTRA), The Seattle King County NAACP, Tabor 100, The Historic Central Area Arts and Culture District (HCAACD), and African-American Writers' Alliance.

Twinkle, Twinkle Little Rat

Twinkle, twinkle little rat, how I wonder where you at?

I thought we was on this ship together captives in a haul in stormy weather.

Now I can't find you anywhere makes me feel that you don't care.

Did you jump ship and leave me here chained to the bottom of this vessel where I don't have the room to turn without creating a wrestle?

Twinkle, twinkle little rat, where you at? Where you at?

What's the problem? Is this scene too much to bear with urine and feces everywhere?

Moanin' and groanin' and cryin' and dyin' smells so bad, and I ain't lyin'.

It's not that I don't care. It's just that I don't know nowhere to place this pain.

Twinkle, twinkle little rat, tell me whatcha mean by that?

I mean, I'm not supposed to be here in captivity.

The Inventors Rap

Excuse me yawl, my name is Lynn; do you know who invented the fountain pen? ...William B. Purvis 1890

I was born a Leo that makes me a lion. I'm glad I got an ironing board so I can iron ...Sarah Boone 1862

Check out a hounddog's ears; see how they flip flop. I bet'cha that's how they invented the mop ...T .W. Steward 1893.

Some call me the pro-fes-sor, and I know who invented the push lawn mower...J.A. Burr 1899.

I got a friend; they call him Big Red, and he can tell you who invented the folding bed ...Leonard C. Bailey 1899.

Hang your clothes on a clothesline wire, or use the invention the clothes drier ...G. T. Sampson 1892.

When I get old I will have made a mint, and I'll probably be using liniment ...Snow and Johns 1890.

I don't think there's anything greater than the man who invented the refrigerator ...J. Standard 1881.

I don't mean to be rude, but I'll catch you later. I need to have a talk with a man about his elevator ...A. Miles 1887.

Come on yawl, let's make a deal. I'll bet you all a soulful meal that you can't tell me who invented the envelope seal. ...F. W. Leslie in 1897.

You just yak, yak, yak 'cause you don't wanna be alone; aren't chu glad you gotta cell phone? ...Henry T. Sampson 7-6-71.

You like the Matrix and the Terminator, both so good they tried to take it and exterminate her. ...Sophia Stewart 1981.

Hold it, hold it, that's enough. I'm tired of all that beat box stuff. Did you know that the bike frame was invented by I.R. Johnson, the electric lamp invented by Latimer and Nicholls in 1881, the eggbeater by Willis Jackson in 1884, the pencil sharpener was by John Lee Love in 1897?

Did you know that George E. Grant invented the golf tee, and Albert A. Jones invented the bottle cap?

How 'bout Dr. Daniel who performed the world's first open heart surgery?

I was just thinking about all the inventions we haven't even talked about: like the invention of the gas burner, shoe sole, curtain rod, cotton gin, rotary engine, stoplights, gas mask, lawn sprinkler, horseshoe, ice cream mold, peanut butter, street sweeper, gas burner, kitchen table, railway switch, railway signals, chamber commode, fire extinguisher, air conditioning unit, fire escape ladder, range, motor, boot or shoe brush, ...just to name a few. Well, all I can say is, these inventions have been invented by Black men and women.

Boy, what an amazing world we live in. A world where we can use our minds and abilities to build a better world for all of us to live in.

I Am African
(Look into my eyes; don't you recognize me?)

She looked into my eyes and I into hers.

Then she said, "I am African."

And I said, "I too am African. Oooh and I have been looking for you!

And she said, "And I too have been looking for you!

How could we ever forget the pain we felt when we were being torn apart from each other's arms?"

Mothers from grandmother's, aunts from sisters, children from parents, brothers from brothers....

And the beat goes on.

Pray tell, where have they taken my family, and for what means have they been taken? My family, My family.

Stolen, Bought, Sold! " I will take your babies at birth and mold them into what I command them to be. Generation after generation after generation, they shall follow my commandments.

Let there be a cry out from the Mother Continent: "Let My People Go! Release their captured minds and let them grow!

Here in this world today I can only pray that we find our way. Lest we forget and say, "I ain't no African and you from my distant land say to me, "You ain't no African!"

Have we completely lost our minds? Have we become so weak of mind that we no longer recognize the relatives that were stolen from our land and lives? Yes, it was long ago, but don't we know that time doesn't erase DNA, that our connection is here to stay, it won't go away!

Shame on us dishonoring our family members that cried tears for our loved ones as they were snatched away from them—our mothers and fathers, sisters, cousins, uncles brothers, nephews, nieces, in-laws, grandparents and great grandparents, and great, great grand relatives. Have we gone completely mad? Look into my eyes. Don't you recognize me?" I am the stolen, bought, sold, your family member, your past and present. How did we forget the pain of such a loss as ours?

My tears are not just for the now but also for what has been and was then. For the millions of us that left our DNA at the bottom of the ocean. Yet, we went on to build a NATION!

I'M SUPPOSED TO BE FREE!

Take a Knee

All Aboard!!

Like the powerful rumbling feel of a locomotive headed towards FREEDOM,

Starting out slow and gathering speed.

Take A Knee, Take A Knee, Take A Knee, Take A Knee, Take A Knee.

Like the sound of a railroad car moving towards EQUALITY.

Take A Knee, Take A Knee, Take A Knee,

I love your determination to be free, but why should I take a knee?

Take A Knee, Take A Knee, Take A Knee.

I realize you've been dehumanized by a system full of all sorts of lies, with false accusations and out and out humiliations fed to the world with determination to keep us down, face down on and into the ground.

Take A Knee, Take A Knee.

I stand accused of not setting you free, but I still see no reason to take a knee.

Take A knee, Take A Knee, Take A Knee, Take A Knee, Take A Knee, Take A Knee, Take A Knee, Take A Knee.

Free to build and thrive, Take A Knee.

Free to be alive, Take A Knee.

Free from miseducation, Take A Knee.

Free from improper incarceration, all forms of misappropriation, including misrepresentation.

Ongoing hateful discrimination, violence and shameful

Take A Knee, Take A Knee, Take A Knee, Take A Knee.

If you stand for peace, love and harmony, Take A Knee.

If you think we should all be free of poverty, Take A Knee.

If the murder of children in our schools is wrong, Take A Knee.

If the killing of Black people should not go on, been done for far too long.

Take A Knee, Take A Knee, Take A Knee.

Make things right and set yourself free.

With Liberty and Justice for ALL!!

ROLYAT MOSI enjoys short stories and poetry. He reads sci-fi, spiritual and religious works. His creative writing before high school was severely hampered by his professional career. Since retirement, he has had a chance to refocus on his desired writing efforts. And he is loving it! *Ole writer with new messages.*

Below is a partial list of his works:
- *The Book of Rolyat*
- *Juneteenth Collection Series*, about the historic fallout of freedom's pain.
- *Black Senators' Profiles*, a writer's display in a Community Art Exhibit for the City of Seattle Department of Neighborhoods Central District.
- *Kwanzaa Collection Stories*, stories about celebrating the Kwanzaa Holidays.
- *Disneyland Bus*, a short play in We Out Here, Festival of Black Playwrights, Mahogany Project's production, Seattle, Washington.
- *African Proverbs*, a production of the African-American Writers' Alliance.
- *Food and Celebration*, video readings sponsored by Seattle Library and a production of the African-American Writers' Alliance.
- *Blackanauts: Profiles on Black Astronauts*, a display in the exhibit The Unspoken Truths: Resistance, Resilience, Remembrance, Liberation, a production of Global Unspoken Truths, LLC.

CONTACT: 206-369-8477 –EMAIL: RolyatMosi@gmail.com

Ali Passed by My Window
Dedicated to my shop teachers

I was just there working, working at the print shop. It was early afternoon on a late August day in LA. It was hot too! We had lots of work over the last few weeks at the print shop. It was now down to the wire on a couple of printing jobs, and I was the one pulling the wire.

The print shop belonged to James Crawford and was called "Crawford's Print Shop." I was pretty lucky to work there and counted it so. There were other folks there that I could learn from including Don, the linotype-man, and Willie Willis, of the Mad Lads. Old man Crawford taught me about relationships and business invoicing. Get that money.

Working at the printing tasks was not a difficult job for me. I brought beyond apprentice skills, knowledge and abilities to the job. I was a production printer. There were things about the job at Crawford's shop that seemed a little medieval to me. I would end up pouring the liquefied hot metal into casts of ingot molds for the linotype machine. Plus, I had the task of recycling old set linotype bar strips into new linotype machine bar ingots in a pot of hot molten metal. That was a little crazy to me. I got to the print shop with the help of Robert Burnett, a teacher at Markham Junior High School's "Summer Opportunity Program" for inner-city youth.

Mr. Burnett normally taught at Washington High School and was well respected among his fellow industrial arts teachers and the 'District.' We, the students at Markham and program attendees, were fortunate to have him come and teach us. I was one of the participants in his class during the Summer Opportunity Program. Mr. Burnett came in with a stylized approach to the "print shop." He had little jobs ready, where we just substituted our name or our saying in place of the next students. These little turnkey projects included personal note pads, book marks, the pledge of allegiance cards, and so forth.

He took us on a trip to Washington High School's Print Shop, where I saw my first linotype machine with my own eyes. They fascinated me, as with all of the machines in the print shops I worked in.

Now, I was originally introduced to printing trade and fundamentals by Bob Schureman, who remains a good teacher friend to this day. It was Mr. Schureman who had introduced me to the beginning instructions for growing trade skills beyond Gutenberg in my early print shop experience. It was also Mr. Schureman that made me acknowledge many important points in my life as I was growing up. His introduction was under the old LA rules, but Markham Junior High School's print shop was definitely in Mr. Schureman's way to young Black students.

Mr. Schureman helped to make the window that I worked in when I saw Ali even a remote possibility of reality's integration. Bob taught me the basics about printing, down to the pica. He took several of the Production Print students on a trip to tour a print shop in El Monte and we had a great lunch afterwards near where he lived in Temple City.

He, Mr. Schureman, also encouraged me to participate in competitive design of labels for industrial instruments and other unique art work. I also learned to make and sell photo albums that I improved on with Mr. Burnett.

It was one of these photo albums with my own work in it that I first took to Mr. Crawford in my plea for work. Now, Crawford was an elderly man when I met him. He was from down south, Marshall, Texas, and didn't play. He was "running a print shop!'

When I first went into "Crawford's Print Shop," Mr. Crawford was busy working and told me he didn't have time to listen right now. I told him that I could help him have more time and he stopped what he was doing and turned to look at me. He stared over his glasses for a minute and then he said, "HOW!"

It was then that I showed him my photo albums with my own work from print shop life at school. I must have told quite a story to Mr. Crawford that day as it must have been amazing according to Don and Willie. They would often have expressions about my talking around the time that Mr. Crawford was hiring me.

I had Mr. Crawford for an undivided moment, and I didn't miss a word in the opportunity to work for him and save him time. He was particularly attentive and when I finished, he told me to put on an apron. Hell, I was hired!! We became good friends and he became a working mentor to me.

So anyway, I was standing in front of one of the printing presses, working hard, when Ali passed by my window. Crawford's Print Shop had a front with two very large windows. They were about 8 feet by 8 feet with an entry door in between, plus another few feet of windows over the top. Over the windows' configuration, in 2 feet high painted letters, were the words "Crawford's Printing."

Mr. Crawford also owned the entire building and collected rents from Blue's Barber Shop, a TV & Radio Repair Shop, a mamas and papas store and the Tobacco Road Shoe Shine Parlor on the side. He was a real businessman!

The printing press lay right behind the one of the windows and the linotype lay behind another window in the first corner front. It was behind this first window that I was working on the printing press when Ali passed my window.

I wanted to run out and join the crowd, the throngs all around Ali (Cassius Clay at the time), as he strolled down the 3rd. I hollered, "It's the Champ. There's the Champ, Mr. Crawford!" I tore my apron off and headed for the print shop front door. Mr. Crawford was there first. He was blocking the door and told me sternly, "You're working." At that moment my focus was on seeing Ali but the immediate experience with work imperatives as explained by Mr. Crawford's presence won the moment.

About that time, Ali saw me through the print shop window glass. He winked and smiled at me through the buffering crowd. That's when I saw Ali pass my window.

Thanksgiving with No Turkey

"Thanksgiving with No Turkey," is about a miracle and a great act of kindness served with generosity. It's about a graced continuation of life and the beginning of a great friendship. It's about how God weaves our cloak of life that we are so warmly wrapped in.

Imagine you are traveling to a distance place to be with family and friends for Thanksgiving Day. Envision your excitement when you are heading a family delegation to join the larger family celebration from your part of the land. Just think when you are stopped in your tracks with an incomparable act giving you a prophetic message. An event of such magnitude, that you are given a message to tell people about. A message that has great hope, joy, loveliness and true holy mysticism that is clothed in undeniable spirituality.

Now think about some of all those you love coming to you and the one person driving losing total control at over 70 miles an hour. See yourself coming to a dead stop upside down after multi-rollovers in a car accident.

Imagine you can even see and feel love ones as they and you looked over the edge of life as wings of angels pad your multi-force roll-over accident within a divine cushion to a sliding stop.

This image became an instantaneous reality for us as we experienced such a frightening car accident on our trip to Southern Cal.

"Us," is a blended traveling family of two vans, with me, Isam, the 60-years plus senior, my daughter, Zena and her two-month-old son, Jazzier, plus two nephews, Imani and Paul, and my niece, Geneva, who was driving. In addition, there was my nephew, Thomas, who was driving his van, and his family, wife Rachael, daughters Recie and Mallie, and my daughter's significant other, Adrill.

We were amazingly blessed, and no one was seriously hurt, not even two-month-old, Jazzier. We were enveloped into a divine cocoon and shielded with grace as there is no reason, we should be alive except God. Even, Jazzier only woke up when his mother touched him to check on him as she sat on the ceiling that was now the floor of the overturned van. It is only then that he, Jazzier, started crying.

Our family was transported by the California Highway Patrol, known as the CHP, took us to the nearby Denny's in Willows, California, whose staff were waiting for our arrival. I know that there had to be some earlier communications from the CHP as the Denny's staff had a table setup for our entire family clan. They and all the customers were quite kind and sensitive to my traumatized family.

Many of the fine folks at the Denny's began to offer comforting words and I felt good and safe. I thought of the great change in our country for traveling black families as I was reminded of my Dad in past drives down south, when I was growing up. We were always told to wait in the car until he checked out the stop to see if it had "changed."

Willows had definitely changed, Daddy!

Some of the folks at Denny's even expressed offers of help such as advice on local sites and driving us to the site of any rental car we might find. In passing by Willows many times before on drives to Southern California, a person of my persuasion might easily picture the small city of Willows as a town down south that you wouldn't expect to be readily helpful, and yet here my family was in the valley of kindness. We were really welcomed and received graciously into that Denny's in Willows, California by all that was there.

But sitting in that Denny's, reality set in as we were now facing the dilemma of getting to southern California to join our family's greatest biannual meal. Because of the Thanksgiving holiday, there were initial reports that no rental vehicle was available for 200 miles around Sacramento.

My brother, Curtis, sent word that we could be put on a waiting list and we're also calling insurance companies as my van was totaled. It was a tense period for us as we were calling insurance companies, rental car agencies and relatives to the north and south. Though this trauma, meals were coming with extra kindness built in from our wait staff.

Then God makes our way as clear as possibly with his angels on earth. Jeannie and Bob Barnes became God's tools who stepped in as angels and said, take our van keys and continue on your way to celebrate with your family, just bring the van back and drop it off at the Willow's Denny's, on your way home. "It's got about 85,000 miles on it, but it will take you there," is what was strongly expressed by Jeannie

Here's how all this really happen, as it is important to understand that Jeannie was becoming varying interesting in this whole affair. It seemed to be her "own" personal Denny's and her "own" investigation.

She came up to me when we first got there as I was having everyone stand to offer a prayer. She asked me, "What you gonna do now?!" at a time and in a manner, that really caught my attention.

I told her that we were first gonna say a prayer of thanks giving to God. I had the family members stand and hold hands as we prayed in that Willows' Denny. Meanwhile, Ms. Jeannie, she faded away for a moment. We then all sat down and started the ordering of meals and the rush of cell phone calls to insurance companies, rental car companies' as well as relatives to the North and South.

Again came Ms. Jeannie, whom I noticed out the corner of my eye. I thought to the Lord for patience as she inquired to me again, "Well, where you going, what are you gonna do?!"

I gather my diplomacy and shared with her that I was going to Southern Cal to join our grander family for the Thanksgiving holiday weekend and then we would be returning to the Seattle area. Ms. Jeannie again faded into the recesses of the Denny's as we continued our amazed visit in the Willows Denny's.

As I was standing for some reason at our tables, again I saw Ms. Jeannie approaching, this time with a huge man, whom I came to know as her husband, Bob. It is then that Ms. Jeannie simply walked up to me, gently took my hand and placed the keys to her and her husband's van firmly in my palm. It is then that she said, "Take our van, go on down to Southern California, enjoy the time of Thanksgiving with your family and when you return, just drop the van off at Denny's."

I was really blown away! I looked at my nephew, Thomas across the table from me and then again at the couple, Jeannie and Bob, who reassured me that I was hearing correctly what they said. We then introduced ourselves and I readily follow Jeannie and Bob outside to their van.

As I walked out, my sister-in-law, Kathy called me to tell me that there were no vans to be found anywhere around. I told her that I begged to differ as I had van keys in my hand. She said, "Huh?" I said that I had met a lady who was loaning me her van to drive to Southern Cal. She said, "Huh?" I said, "I'm with her now and I have to go," as I was walking to the van. I hung-up and Jeannine and Bob had me inspect their van. I just couldn't believe what I was doing and what was happening.

Our family delegation was able to continue on to Southern California with no mother crying, no one in the hospital or blood or injuries. In an accident that was the baseline ingredients for broken necks, broken bodies and death, there was none. There were no major issues to be found in our blessing of grace. We were able to travel on because of a great act of random kindness in a van with angel's wings.

We were still able to enjoy a wonderful meal and just kept sharing God's message of grace with great thanks with all we met. All found the tale to be of great comfort and astonishment. Some exclaimed it was unbelievable but none stopped eating!

We were all blessed to still have a great Thanksgiving weekend. Our plans went well and no other incidents of issues to report. My grandniece, Mallie, Thomas' daughter, still got to go to Disneyland for her fourth birthday with her family. My oldest sister, Diara, had her dinner for Georgia.

Northwesterners went to Hollywood, California Beaches and other sites. We all had a grand reunion over the weekend, and everyone was held and loved including young Master Jazzier, who was held by many.

After Church on Sunday, we gathered to leave at my sister Sheldred's home. My niece, Geneva drove north out of Los Angeles through the Grapevine into the valley below. My brother, Curtis with his son-in-law Emory, drove south from Seattle to meet us with a rented van.

We met in Willows at the Denny's, where we return the van keys to our angels, Jeannie and Bob. We had a moment of joy and celebration and true thanksgiving. Then we headed back on the road to continue on to the Great Northwest for the Puget Sound.

We were blessed with grace to be home and we are all well, safe and amazingly blessed. The prayers of all of us and our forefathers have moved the heart of the Lord, who saw fit to show us his power and majesty along with a blessing of compassion and restoration. God only wanted the van and took it at 70+ miles an hour, while my niece, Geneva, drove. I pray that all who experienced and witness this event also share their testimony with all they come in contact with.

Concrete Roses

Piercing asphalt and raising the indomitable human spirit in us from a cultural seed. We strive for what we came for, knowing where we come from. Will you yearn for what we want? Please see the Creator. It is the Spirit in us, we are spirits encased in earthen vessels. We joined Earth from falling precipitation of the universe, the Stardust sprinkled into each of us with an ember of eternity given by the Creator, for us to breathe upon this earth. It is this galactic dust and breath of God we are, we all are.

We are what we are and grow as concrete roses splitting asphalt furrows. It is like a foot path to a garden, piercing the very essence of the car on asphalted rocks. Our growth goes on to bear the weight of tires on the cars and feet of the people while remaining as a stub of grass in the middle of the street. We claw at life and are fine in every pause of the beats of our hearts.

We are our own cinder blocks, stacked up on each other to the heights of eternity bringing the road up to a pathway in the sky. And between us is the mortar of love that continues to take us on high. In all, we do as we create an arch with many Keystones, each having its own thought, each having its own emanation, each having its own brilliance and its own creation.

Our roots reach down to concrete weaving between the rocks as branches that shatter glass ceilings into shards of hope. Our leaves unfold unto views never before beheld as they are our own creations. Even the granite pillars cannot stop our growth, for on top of each is a capstone of new hope.

Our fragrance mixed with the industrial smoke and waste. Our nostrils fend off the stench that we passed through each day as arms touch everything in every way. Weeds grow despite all that falls down the hill below and seeks to contaminate the very rolls that our feet are entrenched in. We cast off pheromones of magnetic culture, which attracts even those that seek to detract.

We are but concrete roses growing in asphalt jungles and unfurling our buds unto unappreciative societies, yet we grow. We grow and grow as free spawn of new stores in minds that are yet unborn. We are concrete roses!

Creator Queen

In all the universe, I stop to positively recognize my mother as my earthly creator. There was a spark of God, an ember of divinity and then there was her. In all the dimensions I knew, she was.

So, before I look to the sky above and stood on terra firms, it was she who held my life. Within her, I bowed down and laid my sublimations to and with her. Within her, I was nourished till I wanted no more.

We were one and there would be no existence without her surrender and sacrifice of her own very nature. She fails me not as I live and sang a rainbow. She is my link to the structure of God in this world. She's the Lord work made into the sacred living writings and I dwelt in her birth sanctuary for my very life.

My world is from her and I first discover me in all of her physicality. With every beat of her heart was a beat for me. The beat still goes on. The Creator Queen has created me.

I heard her hymns vibrating along my umbilical connection in my world she created for me. I knew the comfort of her soft hums at night and the brightness of her tunes in the morning.

The first sky I knew was the ceiling of her womb. My speech grew from her talks resonating a voice within to my world. I listen to her songs she rhythmically spun from her voice box and stilled the waters in my soul.

From the basement of my soul to the rafters of my thoughts, there she is. I was created from her binary operation that produced me and thrust me into a new world.

She is the feminine divine. She is the Queen of my soul. She is the Creator Queen. She is my Mother, Queen of my creation.

Annual reading at Elliott Bay Book Co. 2020

Margaret Barrie

Helen Collier

Jaye Ware

Gaylloyd Sissón

MERRI ANN OSBORNE has been an AAWA member since 2017. Stories and storytelling have intrigued her since childhood. Living and travelling abroad inspires her to write stories exploring the intersection of culture, history, class, nature, and social issues through multi-genre writing styles. Her first published short story, "The Crew," appeared in AAWA's 2018 anthology, *Voices That Matter*.

City Girl, Country Summer, a middle grade historical fiction novel, is planned for publication in 2022, and she is working on a compilation of short stories for a 2023 publication date. Merri Ann is also an actor and the Executive Director of the arts organization the Mahogany Project. www.mahoganyproject.org.

Khadijah Jordan illustrated Zahara Goes to Summer Camp and Chino Gonzales provided the graphic design for Humidity.

Unrecognizable

This narrative poem is inspired by the African proverb, "He that beats the drum for the mad man to dance is no better than the mad man himself."

Smoke from the bonfire reaches towards the sky, erasing the beauty of the setting sun.

I'm surrounded by mask-less neighbors and friends who I don't recognize anymore.

Even my parents, standing next to me, their faces once filled with love, are now like the others.

Unrecognizable.

Before, I could swallow the medicine they would give me. Trusting them, feeling better soon after.

But now?

Mom and Dad want me to believe in the man that is speaking, to hear his words and follow him.

I'm here. With them. Listening.

And I'm afraid. Afraid for them. Afraid of them.

The medicine this man is dispensing, his words and actions they want me to ingest, without question?

I can't!

But I'm here.

He's talking from the podium. My parents and others in my town are calling him our leader, our savior.

As he talks, his words, like a magician's sleight of hand, hypnotizes and enchants.

Casting a spell on the crowd.

Joking with us, he stands there, like he knows us. He acts like he's one of us.

But he's not one of us.

And I don't want to be like him.

But I'm here.

What if my friends from school saw me here? Would they look at me differently? Would they listen to how I really feel, what I truly think?

Would they see ME?

Could I lose their friendship forever?

He is saying the names of people he used to call friends. But now he is calling them enemies and cowards.

How does a friend become an enemy?

Could I be his enemy one day?

I'm confused.

The crowd is swaying back and forth to his words. Yelling, clapping, and chanting his name.

Swallowing the encouraging shouts from the crowd, he puffs out his chest; back straight he stings stronger.

He's taking over our bodies, our minds, our souls, our good intentions.

Power being drained from us to him.

We surrender, willingly.

He throws a book into the bonfire he calls the constitution and then another he calls laws.

They disappear into a puff of smoke and those around me chant his name louder.

Do the others feel peace and joy from his words?

I feel fear.

Afternoon turns to night.

When the man leaves to talk again in another town, others take his place on the podium. Indistinguishable from each other, they spew, accuse, damn, and threaten.

I try to block out their words.

I want to become invisible.

I must get out of here!

But where would I go? What would happen to my family?

My leaving could get them branded as traitors from those who stand here now. Family and friends armed with weapons of war.

Am I willing to risk that?

To survive, is my only option to blend in with this faceless crowd of hurt and hate?

How long would I have to wear such a mask?

What if I become unrecognizable to myself?

I stare into the flames, praying for a sign to break me free from this madness!

Zahara Goes to Summer Camp

Spring had come to the city
The flowers were in bloom
Little Zahara loved springtime,
Especially when walking to school

She took her time to wave
At squawking birds in the trees,
Admiring the colorful roses,
Their scent floating in the breeze

She didn't mind bugs and bees,
Pollen in the air
In Kiswahili, "Zahara" means flower, bloom, and shine
She felt magic everywhere

And far off in the distance,
Mt. Tahoma full of snow
Made her feel so special
Her body aglow

At school she liked reading
and writing,
Math, spelling, music and art,
Hanging out with friends,
And playing in the park

She gave thanks every day
For the food she had to eat
Thankful for her parents and big brothers
Even the shoes on her feet

But when spring ended
With summer just beginning
Her parents told her something she didn't expect
That set her mind a'spinning

"We signed you up for summer camp," said Momma
Zahara listened, stunned
"Hiking, canoeing, swimming,
You'll have so much fun"

"I went to camp when I was your age"
Her daddy added in
"I remember all the laughter
At the campfire with my friends."

Zahara loved her parents
Always did what she was told
But she didn't want to go to some boring camp
She quickly told them so

Zahara started pleading
To her mother and her father
"Please don't send me to summer camp
I won't be a bother

I'll clean the house, I'll do any chore
Please let me stay AT home!
Don't send me off to summer camp,
I'll feel so alone."

Momma told her gently
"It's just for a week.
And baby you won't be all alone
There are lots of kids you'll meet

Trust me, Zahara, when I say,
Don't worry so
We know you'll have so much fun
You'll be glad we let you go"

Daddy said, "When you come home from camp
Oh, the stories you'll have for us,
In fact, I could use a summer camp

You're kind of making me jealous!"

She still wasn't convinced
So, that night before she went to bed
Zahara told her brothers
This is what the second oldest said

"Little sis, don't worry,
No need to be so sad
Hiking, canoeing, and swimming,
That camp doesn't sound so bad

At least you'll be having fun
Listen to what Dad has us doing
Weeding, painting, fixing stuff
WE sure won't be canoeing"

"You're right about that!" her oldest brother laughed
But, Zahara, don't you know?
Your camp is near Mt. Tahoma
Now, I bet you want to go!"

He was right! Now she was excited
Let me tell you why
She wanted to see Mt. Tahoma up close
Under the big blue sky!

The next few weeks Daddy told her
Stories of when he was young
When he went to his first camp at eight years old
How much he changed when it was done

"You're eight, just like I was
It's your first time away from home
Feeling lonely and even scared,
Maybe thinking you won't belong?

But listen closely, Zahara,

To what I'm telling you
Just be yourself, know you are loved
You'll be surprised what you can do."

The night before she left for camp
Zahara checked if she had everything
Toothbrush, toothpaste, pajamas
Hairbrush, towel, and swimming suit
Long pants, shorts, and shirts
Sandals and walking boots
Hat, jacket, and raincoat
Underwear and sunblock
So many things to remember
Could there be something Zahara forgot?

The next morning, she hugged her family
And got on the summer camp bus
Trying not to feel so lonely
Trying not to feel so lost
When they arrived at the camp
Everyone was moving in a blur
Kids, teenagers, and adults
There was excitement everywhere

Her wooden cabin was named Chinook
Like the salmon that swim so strong
There were five bunk beds, which meant ten little girls
She hoped they would all get along

Zahara's bed was on top
She never slept in a bunk bed before
She hoped she wouldn't fall off
And roll hard onto the floor

Just then she heard a bell ringing
She put her suitcase down
And ran outside to see what was going on
Why they were making that sound

The bell let everyone know
That summer camp had begun
From that day, when that bell rang,
It meant it was time to have fun

The counselors talked about safety
She tried to learn everyone's name
They ate lunch together, under the trees
And played fun camp games

Always there, peeking up from between the trees
Come to save the day
Was Mt. Tahoma, her dear old friend
And she knew she'd be okay

The first night at the campfire
They learned about the stars
Like The Big Dipper and the Milky Way
With binoculars she saw Mars

In her bunk bed that evening
She giggled with the other nine girls
They laughed about all they did that day
And then something flew into her curls

She couldn't help it; she started itching
and swinging her arms in the air
Bug spray, that's what she forgot
As mosquitoes buzzed in her ears

Then the counselor came and yelled
"Lights out; it's time to go to sleep"
He closed the door, everyone got quiet
And soon she was sound asleep

On day two she made more friends
Saw a deer, an eagle, and a hawk

They learned how to be good leaders
And not be afraid of the dark

Day three they went hiking in the forest
Full of hemlocks, spruces, and pines
The forest helped her feel so calm
That she lost all sense of time.

In the afternoon they went canoeing and swimming,
In a cool mountain lake
She had never rowed before in her life
That night she felt her arms ache

But she couldn't wait to canoe
The next day and the next day again
The days were passing by quickly
Soon they would come to an end

And every morning when she woke up
She saw the mountain, oh so high
It gave her strength, hope, and joy
She felt like she could fly

On the fourth day, sitting at the campfire
She told a scary story she'd learned from her dad
And when she said "Boo" on the final line
Her counselor fell, frightened off his chair!

Day Five the campers met the national park rangers
Who let them wear their ranger hats
And told the kids they were the future
For keeping the forest intact

"The mountains, animals, trees, fish, and water,
Insects and the air
All must be treated kindly," they said
"Please give them lots of care

It doesn't matter what age you are,
There's plenty you can do
Living in harmony with nature
Makes a healthy world for me and you."

When Day Six came she cried silently
Zahara knew she would soon be home
And while she missed her family
She knew that she had grown

Just like her daddy had told her
Something inside her had changed
She now trusted and believed in herself
And no longer was afraid

Day Seven, the final one at the camp
She exchanged phone numbers with her new friends
The campers had come from all over Washington state
They promised to meet again

When she got home that night
Back together with her family
Zahara told them camp stories
The beauty of the trees

Hiking, swimming, and canoeing
Mt.Tahoma and the animals she had seen
How she wanted to become a camp counselor
When she became a teen

Zahara was true to her name
That summer she shined and blossomed
Hiking, swimming, and canoeing
Zahara, you are

AWESOME!

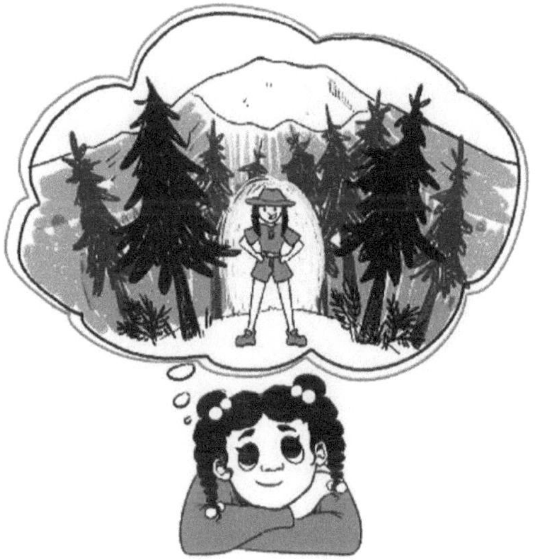

Humidity

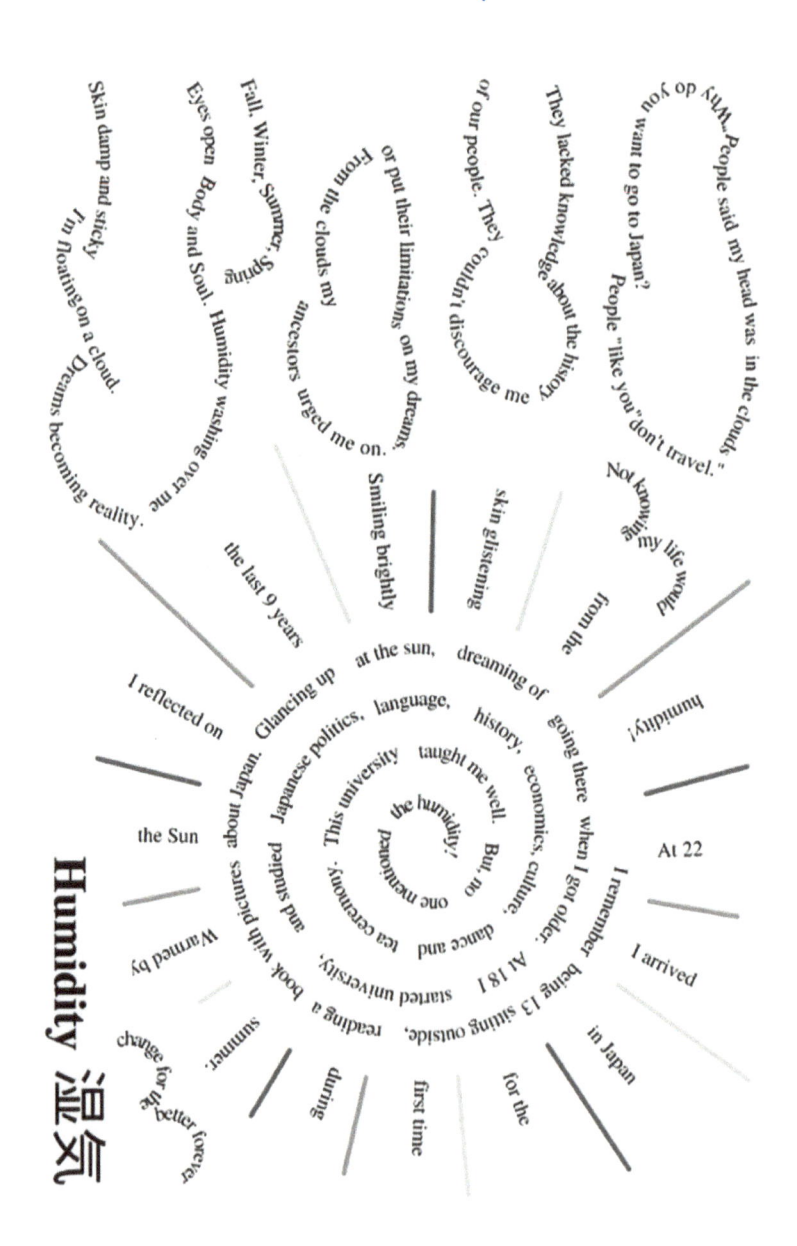

People said my head was in the clouds. "Why do you want to go to Japan? People 'like you' don't travel." They lacked knowledge about the history of our people. They couldn't discourage me or put their limitations on my dreams; my ancestors urged me on. Smiling brightly, skin glistening from the humidity! Not knowing my life would change for the better forever.

At 22 I arrived in Japan for the first time during summer. Warmed by the Sun I reflected on the last 9 years. Glancing up at the sun, dreaming of going there when I got older. At 18 I started university, reading a book with pictures and studied about Japan. Japanese politics, language, history, economics, culture, dance and tea ceremony. This university taught me well. But no one mentioned the humidity!

Fall, Winter, Summer, Spring. Eyes open Body and Soul. Humidity washing over me. Skin damp and sticky. I'm floating on a cloud. Dreams becoming reality.

Humidity 湿気

Annual reading at Elliott Bay Book Co. 2020

Alliniece Andino

Helen Collier

Georgia S. McDade

Gaylloyd Sissón

LOLA E. PETERS is semi-retired from a 40-year plus career as an organizational development and training professional. She serves as editor-at-large for the South Seattle Emerald and has written for many other publications. She lives in West Seattle where she writes essays, poems, and short stories that reflect her commitment to justice. She has published two collections of poems, *Taboos* and *The Book of David: A Coming-of-Age Tale*, as well as a book of essays, *The Truth About White People*.

Lola has been a proud member of Seattle's African-American Writers' Alliance since 2007 and has served on various boards including Central Area Motivation Program, Technology Access Foundation, Leadership Tomorrow, and Onyx Fine Arts Collective. View her website (www.lola-e-peters.com) for more information, including a list of her published articles and access to her blog.

Never Ending
(Inspired by the sculpture by Earnest Thomas)

Our feet planted
on this iron rock
we look to the sky
to view what our sun
chooses to illuminate
Knowing our souls call us
beyond these feeble limits
to follow the steely determination
of our imaginations
Until we find the source
of our waking dream.

Grace

You drove me deep,
deep down
into the well
'til my pleading eyes
were out of your sight
and the wail of my spirit
beyond your hearing.
You did not know
the walls were made
of gold
and the sweet river
of Life
ran below.

My Space

Where is the holy place
The place where brown-skinned people can stand tall
Without huddling
Where black-skinned people can speak Truth
Without whispering
Where tears flow from tenderness
And not rage
Where all that's seen can be told
Without fear
Where laughing eyes belong to adults
As well as children
Where a gentle spirit
Can find peace?
Where is that holy place?
When I find it, it will be my space.

A Lost Diamond of the Patriarchal Society
(Inspired by the encaustic painting by Jeremy Bell)

You covered me in darkness
Unaware
The moon and stars
Became my playmates

You took away the sunlight
Not seeing
My Roots growing
Beneath your feet

You separated me from sight
Oblivious
I fomented revolution
In the shadows

Just because
You can't see me
Doesn't mean
I'm not there.

Spring Blossoms

Recognize the fallow time
when nothing happens above ground
as earth feeds seeds in darkness
and earthworms turn detritus from the active seasons
into mulch and peat and dirt

Does the seed despair of the blackness that surrounds it?
Does it fear transformations happening within?
Is it aware there is possibility in its future?
Can it tell what it will become?

Then comes that violent moment
The seed bursts and life surges upward against gravity
Forces its way toward the sun
Pushes the darkness out of its way
Losing part of its protective coating
Unsure what the consequences will be
Aware it can no longer stay confined in comfort
Proclaims itself a new thing upon the earth

We smile at the crocus or the daffodil
not comprehending the revolution
behind its birth
Dangerously diminishing
the potential of our own insurgency.

Prequel

Who doesn't love The River
Bustling, caroming, lollygagging, drifting
Nurturing the willow with the tadpole
And the daffodil with the crocodile
Coursing through valleys
Jumping down gulches
Leaping over canyon walls
Carrying dreams of generations?

But who is it that loves The Blizzard
Stopping us in our tracks
Impeding commerce
Inconveniencing our daily plans
Adding snow to the mountaintops
Building frozen lakes that nurture headwaters
Until Spring's warm breath sets them free
To become The River?

Breathe, Children, Breathe

Breathe, children, breathe

Stars swirl round my apron
spun dust-like
from the first Drumbeat
of Life

Breathe, children, breathe

Dance with me
between the miniscule luminous orbs;
recall the magnificence suspending them
reclaim its profound beauty

Breathe, children, breathe

Gaze into the moonless night
See the Black beauty of all birth
clinging to my skin in layers
deeper than Time's memory

Breathe, children, breathe

Behold the orgiastic ebony energy
that powers all light
manifesting thought into being
faith into biology

Breathe, children, breathe

Close your eyes, come close
Remember before the dream,
before flesh and bone
we were one

Breathe, children, breathe.

Night is your name for me
Day is your infinitesimal illusion
Take off the mask
See me so you can finally see yourselves

Breathe, children, breathe

Inside the Cave
for Georgia Stewart McDade, Ph.D.

Inside the cave
We sit in dark stillness
afraid
alone
restless
whispering incantations of Liberty
scratching symbols in oblivion
startled by unidentifiable sounds
tempted by curiosity

Suddenly
Thunder speaks:
    Publish or perish, I always say
    We have to help EACH OTHER; don't you know
    Our voices NEED to be heard
    I don't think SHAKESPEARE worried if anyone liked his work

The guard rock shatters
Light streams through the fissures
We stand among multitudes
Our ciphers resonate as fire and air and water and earth
Nourishing as we have been fed
Liberating as we have been freed

Thunder sighs.
Her work is satisfied
Seeds are deeply rooted
Words will sprout
Outside the cave.

Branded
(Inspired by the painting Her Royal Highness, Queen Nancy Green by Robert L. Horton)

Blackness
is the Invisibility Cloak
under which
I wield my potency

Keep staring at my form
and I will
take your substance
to weave the power
of my generations
Leaving you sleeping
in abject moral poverty

See subjugation in my clothing
missing the wefts of lived wisdom
woven between the warp yarns
drawn from ancestral knowledge

Take nourishment from my hands
without tasting the antidote to hate
ground, powdered, and mixed within

See what you want
Know what you will
Anthropologists will one day dig my image
from your refuse piles
and recognize the queen that I am.

Dark Matter

We are
the Black firmament
of all Beginnings
birthing stars and moons
planets and comets

We are the force
holding celestial reality
in suspension with imagination
sparking life from the collision
of aspiration and determination

We are the force
focusing thought into action
squeezing reality out of dreamtime
revealing life disguised as endings
carving paths through shifting sands of memory

We are the force
between letters and words
notes and melodies
numbers and formulas
quarks and beings

We are the force
coaxing seeds beyond their shells
singing buds into blossoms
dancing fields into universes of life
feeding the planet

We are the unseen
the unacknowledged force
holding meaning in place
birthing reality from fantasy

We are the force

nurturing nations' souls
with music, dance, art, and theater
nourishing the world
with kernels carried from ancestral memory

We are the Dark Matter
binding Time to Space
defining the existence of all things
animating the inanimate

Our extinction
signals the unraveling
of universes
seen and unseen

We are the force

ReEvolution

So it is we come again
to the fork
between extinction or change

History holds out hope and despair
generations electing competitive wars
generations choosing collaborative peace

Can we redefine winning
    to bring wholeness
Will we re-envision power
    to empower community
Do we see paths forward
    to create a new reality

We whose footfalls drum the Earth
and hearts beat to her song
Whose eyes see future generations
and ears hear stories yet unspoken

We who feel the Universe's breath
whispering wisdom from multitudes of ancestors
Who have stayed behind
to till the soil and clean the watery veins

We are the Tenders
finding our way back
making ways out of no way
building connections
where they have been broken
by greed and domination

We are the Re-evolutionaries
inviting earth to join the chorus of the universe
Let go the ways leading back to nowhere
Take the path to the new way of Human Being
Join the new Dance of Life

DELBERT RICHARDSON is a Community Scholar, Ethnomuseumologist, and Second Generation Storyteller, of the National Awarding Winning American History Traveling Museum: The "Unspoken" Truths. With the use of authentic artifacts, storyboards, and the ancient art of "storytelling," Mr. Richardson teaches "American History" through an Afrocentric lens. His work is broken into four sections: Mother Africa: which focuses on the many contributions by Africans in the area of science, technology engineering, and mathematics (S.T.E.M.), American Chattel Slavery: the brutal treatment and psychological impacts on African Americans of the Diaspora, The Jim Crow era: The racial caste system that focused on the creation and enforcement of legalized segregation, and Still We Rise: which focuses on the many contributions in the Americas; Black inventors/inventions.

Mr. Richardson's work is primarily geared towards k-12th grade students as well as professional development training for (primarily) white female teachers that make up over 79% of the national teaching force. D.E.I. (diversity/equity/inclusion) training is also a part of Mr. Richardson's portfolio.

Mr. Richardson's work is primarily geared towards K-12th grade students as well as professional development training for (primarily) white female teachers that make up over 79% of the national teaching force. D.E.I. (diversity/equity/inclusion) training is also a part of Mr. Richardson's portfolio.

His awards include:
- 2021 Governor's Arts & Heritage Spotlight Award
- 2021 Museum of History & Industry (MOHAI) History Makers
- 2019 City of Seattle, Mayor's Arts Award
- 2019 Crosscut Courage in Culture Award

We Gonna Be Free

WEZ GONNA BE FREE
Wez have no property.
Wez have no wives
BUT WEEZ A GONNA BE FREE!
Wez have no city
Wez have no country
BUT WEZZA GONNA BE FREE!
You made us give up our language
You made us give up our customs
BUTS WEZZA AGONNA BE FREE
You even had the gall to take away our drums
You raped my mother
You castrated my father
You sold my siblings
'BUT WEZZA GONNA BE FREE

My spirit and my soul will forever be connected to Mother Africa
Which means I'll always be free.

When All Lives Matter

ALL LIVES MATTER WHEN BLACK LIVES MATTER.
Have you heard the news? HAVE YOU HEARD THE NEWS...ALL LIVES
      MATTER WHEN BLACK LIVES MATTER!
IS LIFE SO DEAR OR PEACE SO SWEET
AS TO BE PURCASED AT THE PRICE OF CHAINS AND SLAVERY?
THOSE OF THE SO-CALLED DOMINANT CULTURE
DID I OFFEND YOU? IS IT SOMETHING I SAID?
WHY DO YOU CONTINUE TO TREAT MY PEOPLE THE WAY YOU DO?
AM I NOT A MAN? AM I NOT A WOMAN?
AM I NOT A PERSON? AM I NOT A HUMAN BEING?
IS IT THE COLOR OF MY BEAUTIFUL SKIN OF CURLY HAIR?
IS IT THE WALK I WALK WITH PRIDE OR THE WAY I SMILE?
I DON'T WANT YOU TO DEFINE ME
I DON'T NEED YOU TO BE DEFINED
DAMN IT! STOP TRYING TO DEFINE ME
I DEFINE ME
HAVE YOU HEARD THE NEWS? HAVE YOU HEARD THE NEWS?
ALL LIVES MATTER WHEN BLACK LIVES MATTER.

Annual reading at Elliott Bay Book Co. 2020

Jaye Ware

Santiago Vega

Minnie Collins

Imhotep Ptah

GAYLLOYD SISSÓN is a vers libre poet, a member of The African-American Writers' Alliance since 2011. The avid hiker and fair-weather cyclist live with his wife and their cat and dog, Sabra and Cheyenne, in Burien, Washington. His writing passion visually demonstrates what little it matters where he writes his gamut of poems, lighthearted anecdotes, and autobiographical commentaries to reflect what he sees as nature and life's meanings. He says, "Poetry guides me toward enlightenment and focuses my thoughts." He sees the past, the present, and the future as three-dimensional realities. Poems help him understand the need to accept pleasure and strife that involve living in a community. Writing balances his ability, he says, to listen before expressing his feelings instead of vice versa.

Spiders in My Yard

Cobwebs in your face
Not created to stop you
But remove pests
You so abhorred.

Designed with beauty,
Intricate circles
Purposely connected a strand
To another strand.

An annoying webbing nuisance,
Established across your path
Between tree branches
And your face

Spiderwebs, not all circles
Depending on spider species.
Some spin tangled webs
Like some events of life.

A Roach

Cock
Ker
Roach

Cock
Ker
Roach

What's
Your
Purpose
Be?

Stay
All
Night

Until
The
Light

Turned
On
For
Me
To
See

You
Scurry
Off

Hid
A
Way

And
Return
To
Stay

My Son and Me

Like our sun's gravitational force and our solar system's center, our school held us as if we were planets swirling through a cosmos. Where I worked, I taught science to you with others attending my class, all new moons in an educational atmosphere designed to bring light to inquiring minds. There was distance swirling around our relationship but later brought us together, me the planet and you, my son, became my single moon.

I was with you during your morning sky crossing, to guide your studies gathered in college and experiences, and watched your daybreaks filled with new ideas in your smiles. And, like the waxing moon that gradually brightens horizons, we now acknowledge our change from teacher's and student's juxtapositions to father and son.

The relationship is a creation where my son loves his dad showing a love-focused light bursting into my heart for an insightful lifetime vision. Son, your love, even though you're half a world away, is warmth that is engulfed by all your actions, all your concerns, all your texts, all your photographs, saying to me, son loves father.

Father loves son. We are family. I'm your proposed role model. My unmarried son, your health and pleasures are my concerns: those women's relationships, your long-range plans, the ups and downs found in life's hard-knock schooling. Free thinking Eleazar. Son loves father. Father loves son.

War

Friday, April 15, 1986, the U.S. bombed Tripoli, Libya. Eighteen F-1s raided the country flying from England to attack Libya as retaliation for terrorists. Yet, here in San Diego at Howe Avenue Elementary School, the staff played basketball, riding toy donkeys. The donkeys wore rubber shoes, and as donkeys are, were obstinate and refused to cooperate. To get the basketball, I had to pull my donkey with me. Jumping off the donkey, or being knocked off, was a part of the game. The game was tiring. Although we lost, with a score of eight to sixteen, we enjoyed ourselves. On April 15, 1986, the morning radio announcer said that thirty-three airplanes were involved in the attack on Libya. Many civilians were hurt or killed including at least eight children.

Enjoy Nature

It's Beautiful
But you're in your
Brand all the time.

There's no way to get out
Except through
Television or radio.

Just sitting outside
The birds tell you
How Beautiful it is.

Yoga

The calm
the breath
fresh air
relax
Peace
be with you
and listen
awhile
Inhaled deep
don't hold
let out
slowly
See the light
inside
of you
The calm
the breath
fresh air
relax

Nature Chatters

Listen to sparrows twitter in
competition with whistling
Robins and
Crow's caws.

Hear the breeze blow leaves
bickering
Eavesdrop when dogs wolf to
each other, and cats express
concerns or purr.

Ignoring nature's chatter—
technology: airborne planes,
auto's wheels road sounds, and
televisions, radios, or cell phones
notifying you.

Ocean Beaches

Find a quiet place
to consume views of Pacific Ocean beaches.

Stand close and listen to the sounds of waves
charging boulders tightly held in sandy shores.

There, seconds until the next crash,
small crabs scurry from predators.

Salty fragrances constantly assault the air from shores of our blue
marble regardless of onshore place.

Changes from warm soft breezes to sharp cold winds
offer the sea's aroma with every taken or lost breath.

The scented air's tactile existence, though unseen,
is inhaled, acknowledged, and taken for granted.

Along rocky cliffs, guardians of the coastal ocean
offer drafts that lift seagulls over shores and along watery
boundaries.

The gulls echo songs to one another
in high-pitched screeches.

On a cloudless day, in the distance over noon's
sparkling sea, near where the sun falls
nothing else but earth's edge challenges the arc
on which the horizon lies.

Admire eastern mountains from coastal cliffs, different colored soil
tattles minerals.
Trees grow dressed in seasonal steel-green.

Other plants sport new leaves.
Flowers in delightful hues thrive from the mountains down to the coast, endeared by the changing weather off beaches,
far away beneath them.

The Weeds Are Winning

It's a war.
Fighting an enemy that keeps coming back
Makes me feel like I'm losing.
Man, against weed.
I think weeds know they're going to win
It's a matter of numbers. There's more of them than me.
But I come out, put on my gloves, and use all the weapons I have.

Life

I think myself a tree.
From seedling to the now.
That's rooted for growth
And maturity.
Each season begins anew.
With springs of dreams.
Summers accomplishments
And grounded autumns.
A tree that lives not forever.
Yet weathered and gnarled.
In rain, in snow, in dryer days
Where rich soiled feet formed.
With limbs that nurture and shadow.
My top lifts toward the sky.
Gifts of life to wait for more
As winters come as a last settled score.

What to Do?

Go back
To where you come
Skin color designate your origins
Go back

Know your place
Gender dominates
The subservient
Know your place

Have nots have not
The money god buys
For haves
Nots, have nots

Haves control education
Media biases
Information and
Money
Haves ignore global warnings
Species decimation
Icebergs melts
Planet unstained because
Global warming
Haves control

Have Nots ignore remedies
Recycling
Composting
Window guarding
Plastic reuse
Have Not's remedies

Extinction

We're still crying
Shock not shocked
The present, still here
Includes what passed

We're still crying
Struggling not have struggled
The fight, still in motion
Includes pass fighting

We're still crying
Standing not backing out
The oppressors, still oppressing
Includes our defectors

We're still crying
Staying on the battlefield
The enemy still fights us
It includes dividing and concorded

We're still crying
Silently accepting name-calling
Those, still separate from others
Includes them found in our ranks

We're still crying
Seems peaceful means evades ability
The successful, still examples are archaic
Includes warless hunter and gatherers

We're still crying
Success, though envisioned, is invisible
The promises, still only reward promises
Includes nature's previous remedy

Extinction

Your Name Is Love

Is there not a day that passes
Where I can linger
Without a thought of you?

Or a dream that can survive your interruptions?

Am I caged, trapped,
Like a wild animal locked in
His own environment, never
To be shackled by the smell
Of capture?

Can I, because of you, die from
An overdose of love and smile
While weeping?

The answer lies between your name
And its meaning.

Everyone knows your name,
Should I mention it again?

But yes, for each time I say
Your name it does not fade
Like a dream, and its meaning
Becomes like a pleasurable fragrance
Which needs to be sensed.

Your name? Isn't it Love?

The following is an excerpt from a work in progress: "Down the Road a Piece."

Arise from the Dead

After breakfast, I usually take a nap on the porch or enjoy an uninterrupted read as I ease the swing back and forth. This morning, Aunt Myra's newly arrived visitor enlivens the living room. She, Dad, and Mom crack up at everything he says.

I slip inside with a soda from the store to find out if what they're laughing about is something I want to hear.

"Come on in," Dad says when he sees me. "This is an old family friend, Jove. We are catching up on the town news."

Jove is lanky and about the same height as Dad, with a light complexion and brown freckles on his cheeks and forehead. He looks like Abraham Lincoln with tight, curly hair and no beard. He wears a dark, too-small fedora and a nice striped shirt. A few of his upper teeth are missing, and his tongue keeps trying to position a set of partial dentures into place while he talks. He and Dad sit on the couch, with Mom and Aunt Myra in chairs across from them. Between them is a small table with cups of coffee, a milk pitcher, a sugar bowl, and toast on a saucer.

"Oh, yeah, Dad. I bet it's old folks talk." I help myself to a piece of toast and stand next to Mom.

"How is William doing?" Dad asks Jove.

"Lordy have mercy, mercy, mercy," Jove answers. He leans forward, chuckling, bobbing his head, and wringing his weathered hands. Everyone shakes their heads as if they know what he's going to say.

"Is it all right with y'all, Emma, if the boy sits right here next to me?" Jove pats the cushion between Dad and himself.

She nods.

He looks me in the eye before he begins his narrative. "What happened to We'yum is somethin' else. Y'all gots to hear every word I say, down to the end.

"We'yum been married to Tammie Mae for comin' on twenty-eight years. She was way older than him and meaner than a tied-up cat. She was right purty when We'yum met her, and he loved her more than anythin'. One thing about her that everybody agreed to is that she was a lazy woman. Some mornings, We'yum would go off to work almost without breakfast, because she told him she needed her beauty rest. If We'yum wanted breakfast, she wasn't gettin' up to fix it, she said, so he could fix it himself. And they lived this way for twenty-eight years, hear me?" He nods.

"After a long day pickin' cotton, he'd hurry home every day to help around the house. If she had gots out of bed, she would more than likely have not gotten out of her nightclothes. The house was always dirty. If he asked her about housework, she'd pipe up, 'Y'all want it done, then do it yourself.' Which he do.

"All around her chair was cracker crumbs, chicken bones, and candy wrappers. She dropped them all day long while he'd be out there pickin' cotton. 'Clean up this mess,' she'd tell him, 'if y'all don't like it.' And when he done did that, he'd fix supper for their three children and then straighten up the toys they left layin' round the house. Lordy, I seen the place myself. Pigs wouldn't live there.

"All the time he be cleanin' up her mess, she be gossipin' about the other folks, like Ella Mae, Jessie, Sally Ann, or the preacher. Sho'nuff, there would be lots to say about them folks, and she be sayin' it."

Jove stops, takes a deep breath, and looks around at everyone. All of us are listening.

"One day, purt near three months ago, after all those years of marriage and when they children were all grown and gone, Tammie Mae done up and died. We'yum felt he needed to do the right thing as he always done. He hired the best criers in town, everybody knows them."

Dad interrupts to explain how professional funeral criers are women who make sure everyone is cared for at a funeral. "They cater to the needs of grieving families and make sure food is brought to their homes. Dressed head to toe in black, they also lead the crying during wakes, which helps mourners express their emotions."

"Y'all right about that, George," Jove says. "The mortician did an excellent job of dressin' Tammie Mae's big old body. She had on a beautiful, brand-new, blue-and-pink lace dress with the fanciest hat I ever done seen. Her lips were crimson red, and her cheeks were rouged. He almost made her look alive." Jove taps his feet on the wooden floorboards to the rhythm of his speech and gestures in the air with his skinny hands and arms.

"The mortician didn't have none of that embalmin' stuff, so it was necessary to have a quick funeral service and burial. He said he was afraid rigor mortis might set in.

"The funeral was that evening, the same day she done died. Everybody was der, sittin' in their pews at chu'ch. The preacher came out and stood in the pulpit above the coffin. While the criers were crying, he talked his head off about how everybody was gonna miss her so much. When he'd finished talkin', different other folks stood by the coffin and testified as to how close their friendship was and all the contributions she done give the community. Two of their children had already started families of their own and claimed she'd been a great mama for them and would be so missed by her grandchildren. When all had said their piece, it was old We'yum's turn to express himself."

"You should know, son," Dad says, "no one should say anything bad about the dead. They may come back and haunt you."

Jove goes on. "We'yum began by prayin' and jumpin' around the coffin. He be prayin' so hard an' jumpin' around so much to prove his love, he closed his eyes and fell to the ground, so that everybody believed his sincerity. He rolled around, kickin' his feet this way and that, and accidentally nudged the table holdin' his beloved wife's coffin.

"Rigor mortis caused her body to sit up with her arms reachin' out and her eyes wide open." Jove stops, stretches out his bony arms, and wobbles side to side, imitating how she must have looked. He stares deep into my eyes and blinks. "Now picture this. That there room was noisy and loud with the 'uhums,' the 'amens,' and the 'yassums,' as We'yum prayed hard and loud to the Almighty God, just askin' Him for one more chance to hug and kiss his Tammie Mae and tell her how much he loved her. Then the room went quiet. The only voice y'all could hear was his.

"Standin' back up, openin' his eyes, and lookin' at the crowd first, We'yum looked baffled. He ain't turned round to see the coffin. Then he does, an' he sees her sittin' up with her eyes bulging and arms stretched out toward him. In the corner, leanin' on the chu'ch organ was a long, thick stick. That We'yum, he picked up that stick and held it high, way over his head.

"'If you ain't dead yet,' he said, 'I'm going to swing this here pole and make sure you is dead.'

"Everybody heard him. Yes sir, everybody heard him."

YVONNE SMITH is a multi-genre writer who enjoys writing to inspire and encourage; she wants to make readers think. She was raised in Memphis, Tennessee. At the age of eleven, the talented young woman wrote and directed her first short play while residing in Freeport, Illinois. At the age of twenty, she moved to San Diego. It was in Glendale, Arizona, where Yvonne has authored articles for online Christian magazines and appeared as an extra in the movie "The Sound of Violet." She has also appeared in other short films in Seattle. Her motto is "Have passion for what you do; do it to the best of your ability; be your own success story." Yvonne joined AAWA in 2018.

Motion-less of Life

I'm just going through the motion of life, like a wheel inside of a wheel
in motion but going nowhere... I'm alive, but not living
Just surviving the mundane day-to-day shallow life inundated with thoughts
That I can't even remember from one moment to the next...
That's how crowded my head space is...does that make any sense to you? Senseless
Words spoken for no apparent reason...sometimes I wonder...I'm on overload
Right now...well, at least my brain is...It's like having a brain freeze
but you didn't drink anything cold... you know
As the night wanes, the sun has said goodnight to this side of the world
And the moon...hello...It's time to shut my brain down...anticipating what
My dream will foretell tonight...I wonder? Well, I guess I'll know tomorrow
If I remember.

When We Were Free

What does freedom look like to you?
Is it the way you think that makes you free?
Or is it what you do?
Are you truly free in your mind?
Or are you still bound by the stillness of time?
Are you truly free from the shackles of our ancestors from way back when?
Or do you slip back in time and re-shackle yourself every now and then?
What does freedom look like to you?
Are you still in bondage to the past, people, places, or things?
Do you really know why the caged bird sings?
When we were free, we laughed together as a people connected in unity
We cried together because we felt each other's pain
We showed each other love even though we had nothing to gain
We were a tribe, a nation, a kingdom... created in the image of the Most High
We were free in our spirits...our souls unbound...free to breathe...free to live
Singing the songs of freedom from the hilltops to the valley low
Our voices in collaboration did resound
And in the fullness of time, we shall take up our mantles
And return to the sweet by and by...our freedom uncaged...unhinged
Revealed...no longer hidden by yesteryears' lie
When we were free... we were free to be who we were
A prognostication of who we are yet to become
Not what someone wanted or conditioned us to be
Reset your mind to a time before time...
And that's how it was when we were free.

What If Tomorrow Never Comes?

Life is busy! We get busy with life...not always living but, alive...in survival mode
Life is just a cycle of repeats...rewinds...do overs...and the world is its remote control
Repeat after repeat...rewind after rewind...do over after do over...yes, just an endless cycle
Do it all over again tomorrow, but wait...have you ever stopped...paused... to think
What if tomorrow never comes? One day we're watching television...rewind...and the next
Thing you know...nothing...utter quietness. The world has destroyed the remote control
The television...never to come on again...no more repeats...no more rewinds...no more
Do overs...What If Tomorrow Never Comes?
Thank God for Today!

JACQUELINE (JAYE) WARE was born and raised in the Pacific Northwest and works in the legal system. She butters her bread as a poet, spoken word artist, and recent playwright. She is drawn to material that taps into social justice and injustice issues with a desire to reach and resonate with the reader/listener. Jaye appreciates the power of the spoken word and playwriting in their ability to impact hearts, minds, and contribute to positive social change. She also enjoys the innocent, light and airy side of children's poetry, prose, and stories. She is on the 4Culture Touring Arts Roster and a long-time member of the AAWA. Her on-location staged play *Madison Park Bench* can be found at https://youtu.be/f4CxxMRO8nw. Her hip-hop pandemic play, *Covid Dreams*, is currently on-demand at https://vimeo.com/ondemand/pandemicplayscoviddreas

Performance venues include Town Hall, Spectrum, Artists of Color Expo & Symposium, libraries, museums, fraternities, courts, art galleries, conferences, bookstores, schools, and festivals as far away as Camano, Orcas, and Vashon Islands. Her work appears in the AAWA anthology *Voices That Matter*.

She believes we should, "Use words wisely. Spread honesty liberally."

About that Love
Being In love can change the way you see things.

"I love you with all my heart.
You mean the world to me.
I've never met anyone quite like you.
I love you more than anything in this world.
I will love you until the sun stops shinning.
I am not perfect, neither one of us are.
Please forgive me of any wrong's I have done".
It still didn't go the distance, ending in a sad blues song.

Wanting can't force a relationship that wasn't meant to be,
no matter how hard you truly were trying.
Unfortunately, when all was said and done,
heart-felt sentiments weren't
enough to maintain a firm, permanent bond.

Tragically, it may have simply been me,
unable to forgive minor slights,
indecisive, spoiled, nursing my own insecurities,
exaggerating flaws; oblivious to my own self-defeating laws.

"I'm not perfect, neither one of us are".
About that love, perhaps the door was only slightly ajar.
Quite possibly, I never met the one I truly loved with
all my heart, who meant the world to me,
until the sun stopped shinning,

A plane could crash,
a boat could sink,
my passion and needs could drown,
I refused to pretend with the painted face of a clown.
Turning sour, bitter while we stumble and fail,
love is too unpredictable and frail,
too delicate to believe two different lives could pull it all together,
    fully commit, completely jell.

About that love you with all my heart,
you mean the world to me,
I will love you until the sun stops shinning -
flattering, lovely to hear, but more was needed to sell a lifetime of peace and togetherness when the tests of time silenced the wedding bells.

Black Identity

Black identity may be hard to explain, look in a mirror and the image is plain.

Black identity is twisted, entwined as an invasive species, systematically woven into the "touch and feel of cotton the fabric of our lives." Stolen lives with swollen fingers pull white, fluffy lint from the boll; pricked and bleeding as sharp ends defend with tiny protective daggers, drawing blood; knowing only not to pick would be at their peril; not knowing the softness of finished fabric, only the pain from picking that never finished. **Black Identity is in cotton.**

Black identity is in the aroma of every percolating pot of coffee. "The best part of waking up is Folger's in your cup." As coffee lovers enjoy their morning caffeine fix, coffee plantations owners were fixated on the bottom line, extracting 12 pounds of flesh, 16 pounds of blood, and a full robust cup of suffering and agony, forcing slaves to grind day in and day out, their only stimulant - a dehumanizing venti sized cup of sweat and tears. **Black Identity is in coffee.**

Black identity is in every salivating sweet tooth from butter-rich pound cake, peppermint candies, molasses cookies, and granny's famous hot apple pie. "C&H Pure Cane Sugar from Hawaii, growing in the sun, island pure fresh and clean, C&H pure cane sugar is the one." The one sugar slaves planted, grew, and harvested: pure cane stalk in Louisiana and the Gulf Coast for trade and export. Their lives and living conditions were far from sweet, but bitter and bleak. **Black Identity is in sugar.**

Black identity is in every ingested and inhaled puff of carcinogen from a pipe, cigarette, or cigar, "Winston's taste's good, like a cigarette should." Slaves only tasting misery. The cancer of hopelessness attacking lungs, aspirations, dissipating in a whiff of smoke as enslaved Africans tilled, cleared, and prepared the tobacco fields of the coastal regions known as Tidewaters extending to Virginia. **Black Identity is in tobacco.**

Black identity is a leisurely stride with confidence and pride across expanse, lush green lawns towards freestone, pillars, and posts; holy ground where ancestors once accompanied George Washington into the White House built by slaves. Now, having picked a Black President, not cotton, now feeling sweeter than sugar, inhaling, filling lungs with pure joy, not nicotine, now with a satisfying morning cup of gratitude and resilience, it is high time to welcome descendants' home. **Black Identity is in the White House.**

Black identity is in Aunt Jemima and Uncle Ben, 100% melanin in my skin.

Black identity is in phenomenal pyramids; accomplishments overlooked, deliberately hid.

A twanging guitar, Mahalia Jackson's voice rising above the stars.

Ringing bells on Wall Street; struggling, hustling, making million-dollar rap beats.

Striving to bury the dark and gloomy past behind us,
choosing to embrace a hand of redemption and hope reaching out towards us.

Black identity slays, casts aside divisions and hate meant to destroy us; led by brute-determination and love molded and made to restore us.

"WE HAVE BROUGHT PEACE TO THE WORLD"
---Harry Truman---

War will never bring peace, no matter how many dance in the streets.

Cruelty shows no restraint,
inflicting pain and suffering at any cost.

Cruelty has no control,
In 1945, an atomic bomb instantly obliviated over 40,000 human beings, many pulverized to dust, radiation injuries extensive.

Cruelty has no concern,
about devastation to the environment, animals, and innocent citizens on the ground.

Cruelty has no compassion, is alienating,
using children and the elderly on the front lines; sorrow and death constant companions.

Cruelty is obsessive, isolating
Wave after wave of barbaric behavior to dominate the planet.
Continuous bombardment causing destruction on an unimaginable scale.

Cruelty is inhumane and irrational,
Over 18 million dying in WWII alone.
At least 8 million perishing during the Holocaust
Packed for transport on trains like sardines.

Cruelty is abnormal, dehumanizing,
oblivious to the insane ravages of war; suffering, hunger, cold, famine.

Cruelty lies and is difficult to comprehend,

torture and casualties high, "kill a German every day," was a Soviet cry.

Cruelty embraces propaganda and enslaves,
hundreds of thousands captured as spoils, prisoners of war.
An estimated 1.8 million Africans captured, died packed on ships for transport during the middle passage; millions more dying as prisoners of slavery on cotton, sugar, and tobacco plantations.

Cruelty distorts vision and easily forgets
preparing for a race war in thanks to January 6.

Matted Queen

Coconut oil works wonders on curly hair, providing much needed moisture.

No one snickered and jeered or asked, "What's wrong with your hair?"
Or shook their heads with a questioning, disgusted stare.

No one said, "Why your Momma don't do something with it?"
Or laughed like hyenas, treating me with disdain, an oddity and misfit.

No one said I looked ugly or called me a lint catching hot mess.

No one pointed fingers, making me feel self-conscious and distressed.

No one enacted laws to govern how I wore my hair, barred me from participating in school events, wasted energy bothering to care.

At home where chestnut, taupe, dark cocoa brown, and caramel bodies looked just like me, I was so happy, joyful, and giddy as could be.

I loved my thick, unruly, and tightly matted hair, protecting my scalp from the intense, scorching sun. Glistening like specks of diamonds from sweet coconut and Moroccan oils; intricate braids, cornrows, dreadlocks, and Bantu knots styled to precision.

The powerful, stunning look of a queen wearing the finest purple silk robe and exquisitely crafted dress, a magnificent crown of purest gold decorated with fine gems and stones meant to impress.

Gliding on air when I walk, a self-assured Cleopatra of Egypt, with head held high, an Empress, Goddess, royal heir, Nandi of the Zulu Kingdom, the Queen of the Nile.

Wise, gifted, clever with a heart of generosity. A mischief maker, loyal friend, a brilliant student given to curiosity.

Running freely in the rain, splashing in puddles, and swimming with no protective cap, no worry in the world, content with my thick as lamb's wool, matted hair adorned with a colorful wrap.

Accepted, beautiful, with a refined sense of pride, wishing all brown girls would support each other with all the positivity they have inside.

As I take my rightful place, a matted revered Queen on an exquisite throne; it is my heart that matters, leaving a legacy sweet as exotic chocolate, smooth as a black opal stone.

Annual reading at Elliott Bay Book Co. 2020

Helen Collier

Minnie Collins

Gaylloyd Sissón

Santiago Vega

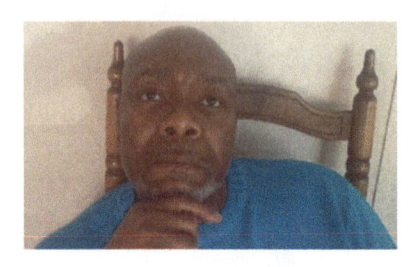

REGINALD "DOC" WILLIAMS became a member of AAWA in 2021. Born in Wilson, North Carolina, Doc writes poetry, short stories, screenplays, and songs. His first screenplay, Black Creek: A Haunting, is scheduled to begin production post-pandemic. Doc is also putting the final touches on Beatific, his book of poetry. He appeared in the short film Emancipation and the docudrama We the People as the Rev. Dr. Martin Luther King, Jr., orating portions of Dr. King's "I Have a Dream" speech. Doc also has a comedic side and was a member of the Los Angeles-based sketch comedy troupe The Rainbow Collision.

His band, Doc Williams and the Groove, performed original songs ranging from blues to jazz, R&B to reggae. His songs can be heard on the music platform CD Baby. His poem "Just Another Dead Nigger" is available for viewing as a short film on YouTube. As a singer, he's also performed with the gospel group The Gospel Explosion.

This Used to Be a Nice Street

Somebody found a baby in the dumpster out back
People used to be proud to be black
Flowers would bloom on the trees in the park
Now folks are too scared to go out after dark
The buildings all graffitied, and most are falling down
When I was a kid, this was the cleanest block in town
We'd get dressed up and go party on Saturday nights
Now they kill each other and it just ain't right
Poor soul he's so cracked, I can see his heartbeat
Damn this used to be a nice street

Let Them Be

Tither and tather they scampered aimlessly about their merry way
Let them be send one to another as they further immersed in play
Time will come when age won't allow such frivolous frolicking, so…
Let them be said one to another as they bustled to and fro

Christmas

Christmas cheer, eggnog, sheer joy is at its peak.
Silent still, winter chill, for some it's oh so bleak.
Cakes baking and people taking
Gifts to one another
Kids play as preachers say everyone is my brother
Stores crowded and girls shrouded
With gifts their boyfriends gave
Our souls have holes just enough left for God to save
Jesus died. Mary cried. "Listen our father," I pray
The price of lice would be our worth if not for Christmas day.

Just Another Dead Nigger

As the tears rushed out of me at Mama's funeral,
I noticed Daddy's face was dry; why?
He didn't express any emotion
As people slowly filed past the casket of the woman
To whom he was married for several decades.
I grew even more hurt when wondering
Does he hear the angelic bells ringing?
Miss Classy, Saints is lying cold and still,
Gone from our touch never to return.
The water spewing from me began to burn
So, I tugged on Daddy's coat.
"How come you ain't crying?"
Bewildered by my inquiry, he said to me
"When I die, I don't want my boys sittin' round here crying;
I will be just another dead nigger."
That set off a trigger.
My tears interrupted for a few moments.
I forgot I was even at Mama's funeral.
But I did not say, "Daddy, you're wrong."
He was too far gone.
In most cases the life of a sharecropper
Wasn't much better than that of a slave.
So why should he think his passing warrants tears?
Believing he's been a nigger all these years,
I felt sorry for him because he felt that way about himself but in the same instant livid at those who created the conditions that allowed this self-deprecation to exist.
I was pissed!
But I sat silently
Almost violently!
A voice from inside me proclaimed
That I was created by the Almighty.
Therefore, I solemnly pledged
To do everything I can
To honor my existence
And let the world know

I was here
This will be clear!
I stood over Daddy's grave.
The offspring of a Slave
Rejoined our Father Figure
The Lamb that was slain.
Is he the same?
Just another dead nigger.

9/11

At 8:45 a.m. on that clear September day
The first plane hit the north tower, and America was in dismay
2,997 lost, 6,000 battered and bruised
As the dust was settling, we knew who stood accused
As the buildings were crumbling and rubble was filling the space,
I watched a man leap to his death; I could not see his face.
I wonder if the Christians and Buddhists stayed apart
Or huddled and prayed together like one beating heart.
I'd like to think Steinberg and Muhammad who never saw eye to eye
Shook hands and forgave each other, and we all know why.
And the last words out of the mouth of the Black woman from HR
who detested whites from the South were,
"Lord, forgive me and those who hate me."
I've come to a conclusion, and this is crystal clear
The closer we get to God our differences disappear.